WILMA
MANKILLER
CHIEF OF THE CHEROKEE NATION

SPECIAL LIVES IN HISTORY THAT BECOME

Signature LIVES

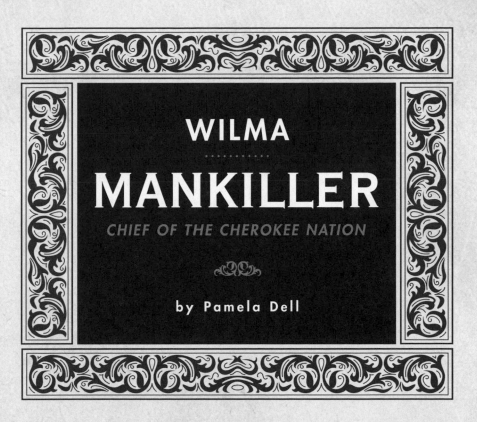

WILMA
MANKILLER
CHIEF OF THE CHEROKEE NATION

by Pamela Dell

*Content Adviser: Circe Sturm, Ph.D., Associate Professor,
Departments of Anthropology and Native American Studies,
University of Oklahoma*

*Reading Adviser: Susan Kesselring, M.A.,
Literacy Educator, Rosemount—Apple Valley—Eagan
(Minnesota) School District*

COMPASS POINT BOOKS ◆ MINNEAPOLIS, MINNESOTA

Compass Point Books
3109 West 50th Street, #115
Minneapolis, MN 55410

Visit Compass Point Books on the Internet at *www.compasspointbooks.com*
or e-mail your request to *custserv@compasspointbooks.com*

Editor: Jennifer VanVoorst
Page Production: Heather Griffin
Photo Researcher: Marcie C. Spence
Cartographer: XNR Productions, Inc.
Library Consultant: Kathleen Baxter

Art Director: Jaime Martens
Creative Director: Keith Griffin
Editorial Director: Carol Jones
Managing Editor: Catherine Neitge

Library of Congress Cataloging-in-Publication Data
Dell, Pamela.
  Wilma Mankiller: chief of the Cherokee Nation / by Pamela Dell.
     p. cm. — (Signature lives)
  Includes bibliographical references and index.
  ISBN-13: 978-0-7565-1600-0 (hardcover)
  ISBN-10: 0-7565-1600-5 (hardcover)
  ISBN-13: 978-0-7565-1796-0 (paperback)
  ISBN-10: 0-7565-1796-6 (paperback)
  1. Mankiller, Wilma Pearl, 1945– 2. Cherokee women—Biography.
3. Cherokee Indians—Kings and rulers—Biography. 4. Cherokee
Indians—Social conditions.
I. Title. II. Series.
  E99.C5M333 2006
  975.004'975570092—dc22   2005025218

MODERN AMERICA

Starting in the late 19th century, advancements in all areas of human activity transformed an old world into a new and modern place. Inventions prompted rapid shifts in lifestyle, and scientific discoveries began to alter the way humanity viewed itself. Beginning with World War I, warfare took place on a global scale, and ideas such as nationalism and communism showed that countries were taking a larger view of their place in the world. The combination of all these changes continues to produce what we know as the modern world.

Table of Contents

Chapter 1

THE TRAIL OF TEARS

❧❧❧

Wilma Mankiller stood proudly in the tribal council chamber of the Cherokee Nation, dressed in a dark suit and a white blouse. She was the center of attention for a large crowd that included friends and family, tribal council members, reporters, photographers, and many other guests. On this day, December 14, 1985, the 40-year-old Mankiller was making history.

In ancient days, before the influence of European culture, Cherokee women had held prominent and revered roles in all aspects of their society. But no woman had ever held the powerful position of chief of the entire Cherokee Nation. As Mankiller raised her hand and solemnly pledged to fulfill the duties of her new office, she officially became the first woman to serve in the highest office of her people. She was

In 1838, the Cherokee people were forced from their homeland in the Southeast and made to relocate to Indian Territory, in what is now the state of Oklahoma.

chief of the Cherokee Nation.

Wilma Mankiller's story is one of strength and determination and hope. But it is not her story alone, for as she herself has said:

> *Especially in the context of a tribal people, no individual's life stands apart and alone from the rest. My own story has meaning only as long as it is a part of the overall story of my people. For above all else, I am a Cherokee woman.*

With this in mind, the story of Wilma Mankiller begins in 1830. That year, the U.S. Congress passed the Indian Removal Act. This act called for the "Five Civilized Tribes" of the Southeast—the Cherokee, the Chickasaw, the Choctaw, the Seminole, and the Muscogee, or Creek—to be removed from their ancestral native lands so that whites could settle there. The five tribes were to be relocated to a vast wilderness west of the Mississippi River, then known simply as Indian Territory.

Once the act was signed into law, the removal promptly began. Over the next three years,

Today the use of the term Five Civilized Tribes is often considered negative and condescending. But the whites of the 1700s and 1800s did not consider it so. By then, the five large tribes of the Southeast had absorbed many of the customs and practices of European and U.S. culture, which the whites saw as a positive, "civilized" thing.

thousands of Native Americans were brutally evicted from their homelands. Hundreds were killed or died of starvation, disease, or exposure to the elements. By 1838, only the Cherokees remained in the Southeast.

That May, the people of the Cherokee Nation received chilling news. The U.S. government was organizing a major military force to remove them from the lands they had inhabited for centuries. Any Cherokee who did not willingly leave by May 23, 1838, was to be forcibly removed.

When the removal deadline arrived, the U.S. troops fell upon the Cherokee villages suddenly and with brute force. With no warning and no time to

The Cherokees traveled over land and by water to reach their new territory.

prepare for the journey, people were dragged from their homes with nothing but the clothes on their backs. Those who resisted being taken were often beaten and sometimes killed on the spot. Old people who moved slowly were sometimes forced along with the point of a bayonet in their back.

The Cherokees were organized into groups to make the difficult trek, over land or by river, to Indian Territory, nearly 1,000 miles (1,600 kilometers) to the west. They traveled west in a series of migrations. The first groups were forced to leave in the last weeks of spring 1838.

Throughout the summer, a burning sun scorched the land. Drought raged, and fresh water was virtually unavailable. Food supplies rotted or were stolen by those paid to deliver them along the way. Diseases of all kinds broke out on the trail as well. Even the strongest soon became weak and exhausted. Groups that set out in the fall had to contend with the frigid winter weather, and freezing ice and snows killed hundreds. Rampant starvation and disease added to the many hardships the Cherokees already faced.

As the Cherokees moved west, their routes were marked by an

As they journeyed westward, many Cherokees refused the U.S. government's offer of clothing and other necessities. This was a means of protesting what was happening to them. Accepting such aid, the Cherokees believed, would send the message that they were willingly leaving their homeland.

increasing number of graves. By March, the last of them were arriving in Indian Territory, the area which in the next century would become the state of Oklahoma.

The trail from their eastern homeland to the western wilderness was a scene of severe human misery. The Cherokees called it *Nunna daul Tsunyi*— the "Trail on Which We Cried," or the "Trail of Tears." Historians differ slightly on estimated numbers,

The Cherokees traveled nearly 1,000 miles (1,600 km) to reach their new homeland.

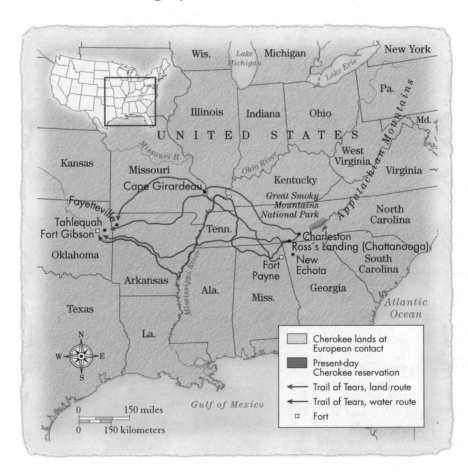

but most agree that of the nearly 16,000 Cherokees forced off their homelands, approximately a quarter died, escaped, or were unaccounted for at the end of the trail.

Those who survived the Nunna daul Tsunyi found little relief at their destination. The U.S. government had promised the Cherokees food, farming equipment, shelter, and everything else they would need to begin a new life. But like countless other failed promises that had been made to them, this one was empty, too. Still, the Cherokees began to rebuild a nearly destroyed nation in an unfamiliar and unwelcomed land. They kept the flame of Cherokee

A memorial in Conway, Arkansas, marks a site along the Trail of Tears.

culture alive as best they could. That flame, and the great spirit of survival, was passed on as new generations were born in the new land. And from those proud and determined ancestors came many future leaders and Cherokee chiefs.

One of the most remarkable and respected of these was born on November 18, 1945, in Tahlequah, Oklahoma, the seat of the relocated Cherokee Nation. From a poor childhood and a troubled adolescence, Wilma Pearl Mankiller would grow up to dedicate her life to serving the Cherokee people. She would become a powerful leader who would guide the Cherokee Nation to a place of restored self-respect and high national regard. ❧

Chapter
2 A CHEROKEE CHILDHOOD

e⌒⊗⌒э

Anyone passing by the house at Mankiller Flats in northeastern Oklahoma's Adair County would not have been impressed. The dense forests surrounding the house teemed with raccoon, deer, wolves, and wildcats. In the leafy branches of pin oaks and hickory trees, woodpeckers and orioles made their nests. But set against this beautiful backdrop, the house itself was nothing much to look at. It was constructed of rough, unpainted planks of wood topped by a tin roof. Beyond the house stood an outhouse, because no bathroom facilities existed inside.

The interior of the house was equally simple. Like the exterior, the walls and floors of its four simple rooms were unfinished wood planks. A woodstove in one of the rooms not only provided heat but was also

Northeastern Oklahoma's Cherokee country is filled with beautiful fields and forests.

used for cooking. The house had no indoor plumbing, running water, telephone service, or even electricity. Water for drinking, cooking, and bathing had to be hauled from the springs a quarter of a mile (0.4 km) away. This was a long way when you were carrying two heavy pails of water.

But none of this mattered to young Wilma Pearl Mankiller. Until 1948, the year of her third birthday, Wilma's family had always rented places to live. But this home—and the land upon which it stood—was theirs. Wilma was happy that her family finally owned their own home.

Like the woods surrounding it, Wilma's house was bursting with life. Her father, Charley Mankiller, was a proud Cherokee directly descended from people who had walked the Trail of Tears more than 100 years earlier. Orphaned at a young age, Charley was sent to an Oklahoma school for Native American children. There, he was made to speak only English and forbidden to use his native Cherokee language. He did well at

Until 1821, the Cherokee language had no alphabet and was only a spoken language. But that year, a Cherokee named Sequoyah created a syllabary, something like an alphabet, which enabled Cherokees to write and read their language. The Cherokee syllabary contains 85 sounds, or syllables, and is very easy to learn because each character represents only a single sound. With the Cherokee syllabary, literacy in the Cherokee Nation grew rapidly. In Indian Territory before 1907, Cherokee literacy surpassed that of their white neighbors.

Students at Native American schools were discouraged from speaking their native languages and practicing their native customs.

reading and writing English, but he did not lose his strong connection to his own culture.

As a young man of 21, Charley married Clara Irene Sitton, a white girl of Irish and Dutch descent. Irene, as she was called, had lived in Cherokee country her entire life and had known Charley for much of that time. Still, they had a whirlwind courtship. When they married in 1937, Irene was only 15 years old.

Charley and Irene Mankiller were in love and happy. Soon they began a family. By the time they moved into their home at Mankiller Flats in 1949, they already had three sons and three daughters.

The eldest was Louis Donald (Don), followed by Frieda Marie, Robert Charles, Frances Kay, John David, and Wilma Pearl—the youngest of the six. She was named Wilma after Charley's aunt and Pearl after Irene's mother. She also had a Cherokee name: *A-ji-luhsgi*, which means "flower." Wilma was an attractive child, with brown hair and hazel eyes. Over the next 12 years, five younger brothers and sisters would join the family: Linda Jean, Richard Colson, Vanessa Lou, James Ray, and William Edward.

Feeding and caring for such a big family was a lot of work for Wilma's parents, but no one ever went hungry. They raised peanuts and strawberries for sale, and they grew beans, corn, and tomatoes in the family vegetable garden. The surrounding woods provided wild onions, walnuts, mushrooms, and lots of other good things to eat. Charley and Don hunted and fished, bringing home wild pig, quail, squirrels, frogs, and many kinds of fish.

Wilma's mother worked hard at home, too, cooking, cleaning, washing, and sewing clothes for her children. Once a year, if the family had enough money, the children would get new winter coats and new leather shoes.

The sizeable Mankiller family had little in the way of material comforts, but for Wilma, it was a cocoon of closeness and love. Her family might not have been able to give her the fine clothes that

Beautiful Lake Tenkiller was not far from the Mankiller home.

some of her classmates wore, but they nurtured her pride and intelligence. She could take these wherever she went.

Their Cherokee heritage was important to the Mankiller family. The family sometimes attended tribal gatherings, where traditional Cherokee ceremonial dances were performed. The dances lasted all night, and Wilma loved the excitement, as well as the chance to stay up late. Occasionally they would attend the local Baptist church, which was encouraged by the whites. But the Mankillers held fast to their native traditions and never truly adopted

Many people enjoy watching or performing traditional Native American dances.

Christianity. To Wilma, except for her own mother, the white people were strange and mystifying. She was wary of them and disappeared as quickly as possible whenever one showed up at their home at Mankiller Flats.

For the first 11 years of her life, Wilma's childhood had been almost idyllic. As a Cherokee, she had learned that all of nature was worthy of respect. She had come to have a deep love and respect for nature—the rocks, the stars, the animals and plants. On stormy days, she loved the sound of the raindrops beating on the tin roof above her head. In the spring, her favorite season, she loved to see the trees burst into bloom and colorful flowers push up from the earth. Mankiller Flats was a beautiful place—one where A-ji-luhsgi, the little Cherokee flower, expected to stay forever. But difficult times were coming. Soon all of this beauty would become a distant memory.

From the time the United States was founded, its government had made many promises to the Cherokee people. In 1835, the U.S. Congress had signed a treaty with the Cherokees that read in part:

> *The United States hereby ... agree that the land ceded to the Cherokee nation ... [will never] be included within the territorial limits ... of any state or territory.*

But time and time again those promises had been broken. When the Native Americans relocated to Indian Territory, they had been assured that this land would be theirs forevermore. But as white settlers pushed farther and farther west, they again began encroaching on lands that had been reserved for the Native Americans.

In 1887, Congress passed the Dawes Act, which called for Indian land to be divided up and parceled out to individual families. This forced the Cherokees, who believed that land could not be owned, to live in ways that went against their culture and beliefs. But

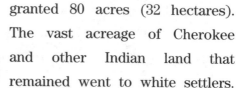
Under the Dawes Act, Wilma Pearl Mankiller's grandfather was allotted 160 acres (64 hectares) in what became Oklahoma's Adair County. This was the parcel of land known as Mankiller Flats. Besides Wilma's family, other relatives had homes on this land as well.

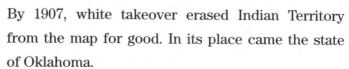

this meant little to the government or those eager to homestead.

Each Cherokee family was allotted 160 acres (64 hectares). A single adult individual was granted 80 acres (32 hectares). The vast acreage of Cherokee and other Indian land that remained went to white settlers. Over several years, the stealing of Native American lands was accomplished through numerous "land runs" in Indian Territory. By 1907, white takeover erased Indian Territory from the map for good. In its place came the state of Oklahoma.

This was not, however, the end of the government's attempts to disintegrate Cherokee culture. In the 1950s, the U.S. government began implementing new methods to deal with what they called the "Indian problem." And the peaceful, happy life that Wilma had known began to come undone.

In Washington, D.C., the Bureau of Indian Affairs had decided that Native Americans would fare better if they were integrated into the everyday life of American society. They set up a relocation program that strongly encouraged—and in many cases forced—Native American families to move to the

A land rush at the end of the 19th century brought white settlers to the new Indian Territory.

country's large cities, such as Chicago, San Francisco, New York, and Detroit. The U.S. government promised to help them move and resettle by providing housing and jobs.

Some of these government officials came to the Mankiller home to explain the details of the program to Charley and Irene. They brought colorful brochures that promoted the relocation program by showing supposedly happy, smiling Indians and wonderful homes. At first, Charley resisted the idea of relocating his family. He wanted to remain in his homeland, near his relatives and close to the land of his ancestors.

But Mankiller Flats, like the rest of the region, had been in the grip of a two-year drought. The family's cash crops were virtually gone, and Charley could barely provide for his wife and many children. The government painted him a picture of a happy family and a decent home in a city full of job opportunities and good schools. The Mankillers faced a difficult decision.

Leaving the life they had always known would be hard for everyone, but Charley and Irene wanted to do what they felt was best for their still-growing family. In October 1956, a month before Wilma's 11th birthday, the Mankillers packed up their meager belongings and caught a train heading west out of Oklahoma.

> *Traveling to California, Wilma had feelings similar to those expressed more than 100 years earlier by George Hicks, one of the Cherokee leaders on the Trail of Tears. Upon leaving the Southeast, he said:*
>
> *We are now about to take our leave and kind farewell to our native land. … It is with sorrow that we are forced by the authority of the white man to quit the scenes of our childhood. … We bid a final farewell to it and all we hold dear.*

Leaving everything they knew, the family traveled 1,500 miles (2,400 km) to San Francisco, California.

Wilma had never been farther than 10 miles (16 km) from home. During the two days and two nights she sat on the train, she cried more than once. As an adult, she remembered that day as the beginning of her family's own Trail of Tears, one from which she hoped someday to return. ♋

Wilma considered the trip from Oklahoma to California to be her own Trail of Tears.

3 EMPTY PROMISES

Chapter

❧

"Wilma Mankiller!" Roll call at school was always painful for the young girl in a new city where everything was unfamiliar and often frightening. Each time a teacher called out her name, the other kids laughed, as if her name were some kind of joke. In rural Oklahoma, where the name was well-known, no one had ever made fun of it. But in San Francisco, Wilma's classmates found it immensely funny that a girl would have the name "Mankiller."

Being laughed at was a new and humiliating experience, but Wilma was proud to bear her family name. It was one of the most respected names in the entire history of Cherokee culture and had been the family surname for five generations, including her own.

The bustling, crowded city of San Francisco was an unwelcome change of scenery for Wilma Mankiller.

In the earliest times, however, it had not been anyone's last name. According to Cherokee legend and history, there were two kinds of *Asgay-dihi*, or mankiller. The first referred to a military rank or position of power, just as the title "captain" did. A mankiller was one who protected a Cherokee village, and each village had its own. A mankiller was a fierce warrior who had risen to his respected position by his own brave deeds.

Another kind of Cherokee mankiller was more like a shaman. This mankiller was believed to have special powers, and his job was to punish those who had done someone wrong. He was said to have the power to make a sick person worse or to shoot invisible arrows at an enemy or wrongdoer.

But in 1950s San Francisco, few if any knew the honored history of this name. It was only one of many painful difficulties for Wilma and her family as they tried to adjust to life in the city. The family had left a strong community and many relatives behind. One who

Each Cherokee person belongs to one of seven clans, or groups of people related by a common ancestor. In past times, each clan was responsible for certain tasks. The Wolf Clan were warriors who protected the village. The Deer Clan were hunters, while the Wild Potato Clan gathered plants and taught their knowledge. The Bird Clan served as messengers. The Long Hair Clan kept and taught the village's history and traditions. The Paint Clan were medicine people, while the Blue Clan were medicine people just for children. The Mankiller family is a member of the Blue Clan.

The flyer

A Cherokee shaman, or healer, was often called a mankiller.

had not come with them was Wilma's eldest sister, Frieda, who wanted to finish high school there. Still, San Francisco was near Riverbank, the rural community where Grandma Sitton, Irene's mother, now lived. One relative living fairly close by was better than none.

City life was a shock for the Mankiller family. They had been promised an apartment by the government and had been given vouchers to use for buying groceries. But they had never even heard of many of the everyday city foods, and there were no apartments ready for them. Instead, they were shuffled off to a cheap hotel in the city's Tenderloin district for their first two weeks in town.

As one of the worst neighborhoods in San Francisco, the Tenderloin was home to drug dealers and prostitutes. Homeless people slept in doorways, and glass from broken liquor bottles littered the sidewalks. Lost and bewildered, Wilma longed to hear the sounds of nature at night instead of fistfights and screaming sirens.

Still, this difficult time offered Wilma many new and exciting experiences. One of the strangest things she had ever seen occurred early on. Standing in the hotel's hallway one day, she saw the wall slide open to reveal a box. Several people who had been standing in the hall got into the box and the wall closed again. A few minutes later, the wall opened once more. Now, entirely different people walked out of the box. This was Wilma's first encounter with an elevator. She soon experienced many other new things as well, including learning how to roller-skate, ride a bike, and use a telephone.

The move to a small apartment in the working-class neighborhood of Potrero Hill improved things—but not much. The space was tight for the large Mankiller family, now with one more on the way, and money was scarce. Wilma's father and oldest brother took work in a factory that made rope. But even with two paychecks, the family barely survived. That first year in San Francisco, 1956, James was born. The last Mankiller child, William,

Children cluster around a collapsed house in San Francisco's run-down Potrero Hill neighborhood.

was born in 1961.

The Mankillers tried their best to build a community with other Cherokees in the city, but it was hard to do. Life was a constant struggle, and there was not even the land to help provide for their needs. Most Indians remained on the fringes of society, often living in slum neighborhoods, with few of the opportunities the government had led them to expect. Instead of escaping from poverty and misery, Charley Mankiller's family found life in California even worse.

For Wilma, life was especially difficult. Her classmates at school looked down on her for being different. It wasn't so much her family's poverty, because others were poor, too. It was the way she dressed. It was the strange accent in her speech. She felt disliked and alone. Much of the time she felt afraid, unsure of herself, and rebellious, with no place to hide in the chaotic city sprawl. So instead of trying to find a hiding place where she was, Wilma ran away.

At least five times in the years before she started high school, Wilma hopped on a bus and rode to Riverbank and the serenity of Grandma Sitton's rural home. Each time, her grandmother called Wilma's parents, and Charley would come and bring his daughter home. Finally, understanding how unhappy Wilma was in the city, Charley and Irene agreed that she could spend her eighth-grade year with her grandmother. By then, Grandma Sitton had moved in with her son, his wife, and their children at their home on a dairy farm.

This change of scene was a positive one for young Wilma. In that stable, peaceful environment, she began to feel more happy and confident. She made friends and started liking herself better. The next fall, Wilma rejoined her family, who had moved to a rough

Rural California brought a refreshing change of scenery for Wilma.

San Francisco neighborhood called Hunter's Point. She willingly enrolled at a San Francisco high school, but she quickly discovered that the inner-city school experience had not improved for her. The school she attended was rough as well, and there were many violent incidents among the students. In class, Wilma felt bored, disliked, and alone. She had no idea what she would do after high school, and her grades were only good in the few classes that interested her.

Wilma never really felt at home in the Hunter's Point housing project.

The only really enjoyable moments she experienced were after school and on weekends, when

she escaped to the San Francisco Indian Center. At the center, in the city's Mission district, Wilma made friends with other Indian teens. Many of them had also come from Oklahoma under the relocation program, so they understood her feelings, frustrations, and problems. At the Indian Center, she enjoyed social events like dances, sports, and just hanging out. It was the place of refuge she had been seeking since she had left Oklahoma.

Still unsure of who she was and where her life was going, Wilma made the Indian Center the focal point of her teenage world. Meanwhile, she waited impatiently for June 1963. For Wilma, that month of that year marked the moment of her escape. In June 1963, she would graduate from high school.

Wilma's involvement with the San Francisco Indian Center helped her adjust to life in San Francisco. It provided entertainment and social and cultural activities for youths, as well as a place for adults to hold powwows and discuss matters of importance with other Native Americans who had been relocated. Wilma recalled, "There was something at the Center for everyone. It was a safe place to go, even if we only wanted to hang out." Though she was far from Cherokee country, the center helped reinforce Wilma's identity as a Cherokee and her understanding of Cherokee history and traditions.

4 FINDING HER CAUSE

❧⌘❧

For the Mankiller family, the idea of pursuing a higher education was about as realistic as flying a spaceship to the moon. No Mankiller had ever gone on to college, and Wilma had never even given the idea a thought. Instead, after graduating from high school, she moved out of her parents' home and in with her older sister Frances. She was hired by a finance company to work in its office doing filing and making telephone calls to delinquent loan holders. And before she even turned 18, Wilma got married.

Wilma had met her future husband, who was four years older than she, at a Latino dance. Hector Hugo Olaya de Bardi, or Hugo, came from Ecuador. To the young, impressionable teenager, Hugo seemed worldly and sophisticated. He had classy manners,

A Native American girl involved in the 1969 takeover of Alcatraz Island publicly asserts her people's claim to the land.

and his dark, handsome looks attracted her immediately. Wilma had barely been out of her own neighborhood, but Hugo drove his own car and exposed her to a wide range of new cultural experiences within the city—people and places she had not even known existed. After a long day at work, Wilma was thrilled to be escorted by the dashing Olaya to a nice restaurant or an exciting dance club. Olaya was enrolled in college, too, and planned to make something of himself in the world.

After a breathless summer in a social whirl, Wilma agreed to marry Hugo. In November 1963, just days before her 18th birthday, she and Hugo caught a bus for Reno, Nevada. With no family members present, they married in a wedding chapel there. Then they took another bus to enjoy a honeymoon in Chicago.

When the young couple returned to San Francisco, they lived with Hugo's relatives before getting their own home. Wilma continued working and took care of the cooking and cleaning while Hugo went to class by day and worked at night.

Wilma soon discovered that she was pregnant, and in August 1964, the couple's daughter Felicia was born. In June 1966, Wilma gave birth to their second daughter, Gina.

Wilma was now most often known as Mrs. Hugo Olaya. Not even 21 years old yet, she had a husband, two children, a home, and a job. But the job was not challenging, and the day-in, day-out routine of her life barely changed. As she tried to fulfill the traditional role of wife and mother, Wilma felt more and more discontented. All around her the city was exploding with revolutionary ideas and worthwhile causes in which to take an interest. People were experimenting with alternative lifestyles and staging protests against rigid university policies, racial discrimination, and the war in Vietnam. The air around her was restless

San Francisco students gathered to peacefully protest the Vietnam War.

Members of the American Indian Movement picketed to raise awareness for their cause.

with the energy of change, but Wilma's own world seemed to be closing in. As the months passed, the stifling routine of her married existence made Wilma think more and more about what she really wanted in life. And as time went on, Wilma and Hugo began to grow farther and farther apart.

In the late 1960s, Wilma took a big step toward the independence she now longed for. She enrolled at Skyline Junior College, in a suburb of San Francisco. Although she had hated everything about school as a teen, she realized that becoming more educated was necessary if she was to enlarge her world. She signed up for classes that included sociology, literature, and criminal justice. She did well and was surprised to find college life much more enjoyable than any schooling she had had before.

Gaining confidence, Wilma transferred to San Francisco State University, enrolling through an educational-opportunity program for minorities. Once she got her footing in this larger, more intensely academic school, she thrived. Soon, she was thinking about the opportunities that might lie ahead, beyond her life as a married woman. She later wrote about this time:

> I wanted to set my own lim-
> its and control my destiny. I
> began to have dreams about
> more freedom and indepen-
> dence, and I finally came to
> understand that I did not have
> to live a life based on someone
> else's dream.

As Wilma continued her college education and gained confidence, her sights shifted farther out into her community. She again sought out the Indian Center, the place that had provided refuge during the turmoil of her teenage years. Soon

As the 1970s loomed, Native Americans across the nation were becoming active in the fight for civil rights. In 1968, an organization known as the American Indian Movement, or AIM, was founded in Minnesota. Its purpose was to bring awareness to the American public about important Native American issues. Chapters of AIM organized demonstrations and sit-ins to bring attention to age-old grievances. They publicized issues such as what many considered the legalized theft by whites of tribal lands and other valuable resources.

she was swept into the spirited atmosphere there and thinking more about Native American rights and issues than she ever had before.

But then disaster struck that refuge. On the night of October 28, 1969, the San Francisco Indian Center burned to the ground. The cause of the four-alarm fire was never absolutely determined, but some suspected arson. Fed up with social injustice, the city's Native American community rushed to organize a demonstration that would get the nation's attention. They decided to take over Alcatraz Island, or "The Rock."

The Rock, a huge stone island in San Francisco Bay, had been used by Native Americans since long before whites had arrived in the West. Later, because of its remote location, the U.S. government had built Alcatraz Prison there. Since the prison's closure in 1963, San Francisco's board of supervisors had been busy trying to find a good and profitable use for it. Finally, they had accepted a proposal to build a huge tourist complex, complete with shopping mall, on the island.

The country's Native Americans objected to its use in this way. To them, Alcatraz was a small symbol of all the North American land they had lost to white Americans. So, on November 9, 1969, 14 Native Americans made their way across the cold and choppy waters of the bay to claim Alcatraz in

the name of Indians of all tribes. This takeover—
and an earlier one that had happened in 1964—was
based on an agreement known as the Fort Laramie
Treaty of 1868. According to that document, any
Native American male 18 or older could petition to
homestead on any unused or abandoned federal land
if his tribe had been involved at the time the treaty
was created.

The takeover of Alcatraz was a highly symbolic

*A group
of Native
Americans
claimed
Alcatraz Island
on behalf of all
native tribes.*

move, and as part of the protest, the occupiers made a symbolic gesture to buy the island from the U.S. government. They offered the government red cloth and glass beads that had a total value of $24. This, they felt, was a fitting offer, considering that white men had purchased New York's Manhattan Island for the same price 300 years earlier.

But they had barely set foot on land before they were removed by the U.S. Coast Guard. Early on November 20, 1969, however, they returned as a larger group. Eighty-nine native men, women, and children again took possession of Alcatraz, this time outfitted with sleeping bags, cooking equipment, food, and water. Over the following days, more and more Native Americans, from tribes all over the country, came to join the protesters.

Wilma's brother Richard was the first in the Mankiller family to become part of the Alcatraz demonstration. Vanessa and James soon followed. Finally, when Linda and her children decided to journey out to

> *The takeover of Alcatraz had a profound and historic effect. It shone a huge spotlight on American Indian issues, causing the American public in general and the federal government in particular to finally take serious notice. It also fostered within Native Americans a new and powerful sense of pride in their heritage and their place within the fabric of the United States. In the end, the takeover at Alcatraz spawned hundreds of other related demonstrations throughout the following decade.*

Some Native Americans erected traditional housing for their stay on Alcatraz.

the island, Wilma went with them. It was a decision that would radically affect the rest of her life.

By taking a stand at Alcatraz, Wilma had become part of a symbolic demonstration that riveted the attention of the entire country. For her, it was a life-changing episode. At Alcatraz, Wilma discovered who she was and where she was going. She had finally found her path. ᕙ

Chapter

5 RETURN TO TRIBAL LAND

೧౿యి

The car was a little red Mazda. It was not fancy or expensive. But for Wilma Mankiller Olaya, it was a symbol of her own independence. She was now leading two lives—one as student and community activist and the other as wife and mother. She was learning and growing. The work she was doing outside her home made her feel more fulfilled and powerful than ever before.

Hugo, however, was not at all happy about his wife's outside activities, and he flatly refused to allow her to get a car. But Wilma was not about to stop what had become her life-giving activities, despite Hugo's attempts to control her. She needed a car to get from one place to another in the city. She was determined to attend tribal events in other places as

Wilma Mankiller (center) is a member of the Cherokee people's Blue Clan. In Cherokee tradition, this clan's job was to serve as medicine people just for children.

well. In an act of defiance, Wilma withdrew money from the bank and bought herself the Mazda without Hugo's knowledge.

The car was a symbol, but its main purpose was practical. Now she had the opportunity to experience many things that she had not had access to before. Since Alcatraz, she had become deeply interested in the changes occurring in society, and she wanted to be a part of them. With a car she was free to go to plays, concerts, political events, and women's rights demonstrations, and she now did all of these.

More importantly, Wilma took a job as the director of the Native American Youth Center in Oakland, across the bay from San Francisco. There she helped establish after-school programs for Indian students. She sought out literacy programs for teens who couldn't read well and arranged field trips to out-of-town tribal events. On top of all this, she found time to volunteer with the Pit River Indians, too.

As Wilma became increasingly involved with Native American causes, she began to see how pride in their Native American heritage

> *The Pit River Indians, whose tribal lands are located north of San Francisco, were fighting a legal battle against the huge and powerful Pacific Gas & Electric Corporation. The tribe wanted to be lawfully acknowledged as the rightful owners of millions of acres of their ancestral territory that PG&E had claimed. Mankiller worked with the Pit River tribe until she moved away from the Bay Area.*

The intake bay at the Pit River Power Plant is part of the land claimed by the Pit River Indians.

empowered her people. She believed that even those living in poverty in the cities' worst neighborhoods could survive with dignity if they honored their cultural roots. She saw that her work was to help increase this pride and to do whatever else she could to change and improve things within the Native

American community.

Wilma traveled often to meet with tribal leaders and elders, and she frequently brought her young daughters along. She began to acquire a deep understanding of international law, treaty rights, legal defense funds, and much more. And with every trip and every encounter, her understanding of the history and culture of tribes native to California and elsewhere increased. Wilma remembered:

> *All of the people I encoun-tered—the militants, the wise elders, the keepers of the medicine, the storytellers—were my teachers, my best teachers. I knew my education would never be complete. In a way, it was only beginning. I felt like a newborn whose eyes have just opened to the first light.*

The state of California is home to dozens of Native American tribes. Among the best-known are the Miwok, Chumash, Shoshone, Paiute, and Shasta tribes. At the time Europeans arrived in what is now the United States, California was the most densely popu-lated of the current states with a popula-tion of approximately 150,000.

At home, however, things had reached a point of serious meltdown. Wilma was devoted to her two daughters, and she wanted her marriage to work. But to give up her new, energizing life would be like agreeing to suffocate. By 1973, she and Hugo were barely a part of each other's worlds.

During the time of the Alcatraz occupation,

Wilma's father had died, and she and her brothers and sisters had returned to Mankiller Flats to bury him in the land of his forefathers. While there, Wilma had felt the pull of the land. Powerful memories of her childhood in Oklahoma surfaced again. She began to think more and more of returning there and re-establishing her roots in a permanent way.

The first step in her plan to return was to leave Hugo. Wilma asked him for a divorce in 1974, and he eventually agreed. She moved across the bay to Oakland, where it was less expensive to live as a single mother with two daughters. To confirm her new identity, Wilma dropped her husband's name of Olaya. She again became Wilma Mankiller.

Mankiller worked hard over the next year. She continued to volunteer with the Pit River Indians, and she took a job doing social work for the Urban Indian Resource Center. She needed to save enough money to make the move with Felicia and Gina to Oklahoma, and this goal was the driving force behind everything she did.

The summer of 1976 arrived, but Mankiller was not yet prepared to move. Instead, she arranged a trip back to Mankiller Flats so

> *The Achomawi tribe is often referred to as the Pit River Indians in part because the tribe's historic land was located in the drainage of the Pit River in northeastern California. The name Pit River came from the tribe's practice of digging pits for the purpose of catching game.*

she could reacquaint herself with the area over a longer time. She found a rustic cabin to live in near ceremonial dance grounds, and she and her two daughters settled in. At 10 and 12, Felicia and Gina did not adjust instantly to living in a house that had no running water. But for Wilma, the weeks in Oklahoma were rich and satisfying.

She enlivened old friendships and took her girls to many tribal events. Ceremonial dances were a favorite pastime. Gathered at the ceremonial grounds, everyone ate the abundant foods of summer, chatted,

Cherokee girls compete in a traditional game of stickball.

and engaged in traditional Cherokee sports such as archery and stickball. The highlight of the evening was the traditional dances themselves, which often

went on until dawn. Mankiller knew she would soon return permanently to the land of her childhood.

In the summer of 1977, with $20 in her pocket and a rental truck filled with her belongings, Mankiller and her daughters made the permanent move back to Oklahoma. She had brought little with her besides a few personal possessions and her unshakable determination to find a way to support her family. At Mankiller Flats, no trace was left of the home she had lived in as a child. But the land was still there, beautiful and rich with flowers, trees, and animals. She knew she could rebuild.

But first Mankiller needed a job. Her mother, Irene, had recently moved back to Adair County herself. Now, Mankiller and her daughters moved into Irene's home. Mankiller immediately set out looking for work. In her free time, she cooked and sewed and played the guitar that Hugo had once bought her.

Finding work was difficult. She hoped to continue her work as an Indian activist, but she was frequently turned down for being overqualified. The long search was frustrating, but in the fall of 1977, she finally met with success. Mankiller was hired at $11,000 a year as an economic stimulus coordinator for the Cherokee Nation of Oklahoma. Her duties focused on spurring Native American college students to study environmental health and science and then to use that knowledge to improve their communities.

Mankiller quickly found that her experience working for Native American causes was invaluable. She excelled at writing grant proposals, some of which led to funding for the Cherokee tribe. Her success impressed Chief Ross Swimmer, the elected head of the Cherokee Nation, and his council members. But Mankiller herself felt bogged down by the slow and bureaucratic way things got done within the Cherokee Nation administration. After all her grassroots activities in San Francisco, she hoped to kindle the same kind of energies again.

By 1979, Mankiller was working as a program development specialist for the Cherokee Nation. She was building a new home at Mankiller Flats and was pleased with the outcome of her move back to the state. But one thing was still undone: She had never finished her undergraduate college degree before leaving San Francisco. That year, she decided to go back to school.

Mankiller eventually received a bachelor's degree in social sciences and a master's degree in community planning from the University of Arkansas.

With just a few courses left to finish her bachelor's degree, Mankiller enrolled in graduate school at the University of Arkansas in Fayetteville, a little more than an hour's drive from home. She planned to get a graduate degree in community planning, a move that

Students stroll across the University of Arkansas campus.

gave her a sense of optimism. Everything was working out amazingly well. She had money to live on through grants and graduate education assistantships. She had been assured that her job at the Cherokee Nation would be waiting for her whenever she wanted to return to it. She had a long drive to school each day, but it was valuable time for planning her future. Little did Mankiller know it as she began attending the University of Arkansas, but very dark days were coming. She would meet them just over the next hill. ✍

Chapter 6

A Brush
with Death

❧❀❧

The night of November 8, 1979, there was a terrible rustling in the trees outside Wilma Mankiller's home. The November winds pushed across the valley, stirring the grasses and the plants. Dark clouds scudded across the sky. But it was not the wind that was creating the strange disturbing noise. It was not clouds that formed the spooky shapes that seemed to encircle the Mankiller house. It was the owls.

That night, seemingly hundreds of owls shivered in the trees surrounding the house. The dark sky was filled with them as they flew and flocked. The owls' eerie voices rose into the dark, chilly air in a haunting chorus.

Where the owls came from that night no one could tell. There had never been an earlier incident

Wilma Mankiller took the Cherokee practice of "being of good mind" to heart: She was able to face death and come back smiling.

of such a thing. But the birds brought with them a sense of foreboding. Mankiller had never been very frightened by owls. But she came from a native tradition that saw these birds as the messengers of bad luck, sometimes even of death, and she knew the stories well. The Cherokee *dedonsek* was a person who could change his shape into the form of an owl, sailing through the night carrying bad luck to whomever it chose. The dedonsek, the bringer of "bad medicine," was someone a Cherokee naturally thought of when he or she heard the ghostly sounds

In Cherokee legend, the owl is a symbol of bad luck, suffering, and death.

of an owl's song.

The owls flocked close to the house that night, and they would not keep quiet. Mankiller went to bed feeling ill at ease. She was not a superstitious person and had no premonition that bad luck was on its way. But why had there been so many owls so close to her home?

The next morning, Mankiller decided to go to Tahlequah, where the Cherokee Nation had its headquarters. She wanted to see about getting some part-time work to supplement her income. Traveling on a two-lane back road, she was only a few miles from home when death suddenly drew near. As her car ascended a hill, she could not see the oncoming traffic. An oncoming car that had been trying to pass a slower vehicle was still in Mankiller's lane. Just as she crested the hill, the two cars violently collided head-on.

Mankiller was hauled, barely conscious, from her destroyed automobile. As the ambulance rushed Mankiller to the hospital in nearby Stillwell, she felt certain she was dying. But the experience was far

> *In Cherokee lore, the owl most feared as a bringer of death was the tsgili, or great horned owl. This owl has razor-sharp talons, a wing-span of up to 4 ½ feet (1.4 meters), and vision that is 35 times sharper than human sight. It has special feathers on its wings that allow it to be completely silent in flight, so that its prey never hears it approaching. These physical attributes, coupled with the fact that the bird is active at night, suggest why the tsgili was associated with "dark powers."*

from a bad one. She remembered:

> *I experienced a tremendous sense of peace-*
> *fulness and warmth. It was a feeling that*
> *was better than anything that had ever*
> *happened to me. ... As a result of that*
> *experience I have lost any fear of death.*
> *I began to think of death as walking*
> *into spirit country rather than as a*
> *frightening event.*

Road signs in Tahlequah, Oklahoma, are printed in both Cherokee and English.

The driver of the other car died on the way to the hospital. That driver, who had also been alone

in her car, was a woman named Sherry Morris. She had been one of Mankiller's closest friends.

Mankiller's recuperation was slow and painful. The front of the car had been rammed so far back by the impact that a part of the hood had gashed her neck. She had broken ribs, a broken left leg and ankle, and the bones in both her face and her right leg had been crushed. During the more than eight weeks that she spent in the hospital, surgeons worked to put her face and right leg back together. After her initial release from the hospital, Mankiller had to return many more times. In all, she endured a total of 17 surgeries and defied predictions that she would never walk again.

But if the owls that had surrounded her that November night were bringing bad luck, all of it had not yet come. In early 1980, her body began to weaken. Soon she could barely use her arms or legs. It was a struggle even to keep her eyes open. It took several months before she discovered what the problem was. She had myasthenia gravis, a form of muscular dystrophy.

The Cherokees attempt to cultivate an approach to life that they call "being of good mind." They try to take a positive attitude toward even negative life experiences and use such experiences to grow and improve their lot in life. Holding to this ideal, Mankiller turned her car-accident ordeal into an experience that helped her later in life. By doing so, she realized that she "had found the way to be of good mind."

More determined than ever to get back to her active, full life, Mankiller underwent surgery yet again, this time to remove her thymus gland. The operation was successful, and she began to regain her strength almost immediately. Now that she had fought and won some major battles of her own, Mankiller's thoughts returned to helping others.

By 1981, Mankiller was back at her job at the Cherokee Nation. Her confrontation with death had left her confident that she could survive anything. With newfound courage and determination, she stepped up to tasks that before her accident she would never have tackled. In her first year back, she helped to found the Cherokee Nation Community Development Department. She was convinced that the best way to restore Cherokee pride was to allow people to accomplish things themselves, within their individual communities. This new organization was created to help that happen. Mankiller became its first director.

One of the first projects the Community Development Department took on was helping the small and poverty-stricken community of Bell, Oklahoma, rebuild itself. The town residents, 95 percent of whom were Cherokee, took the improvements into their own hands and greatly revitalized their community. With Mankiller's guidance, they refurbished old homes and built

25 solar-powered homes. They laid 16 miles (26 km) of water pipeline, bringing running water to many homes for the first time. The community effort was so successful that it received national media coverage—including a "before and after" story on CBS news.

Tahlequah, Oklahoma, is home of the Cherokee Nation headquarters.

Mankiller could not have been more proud to see her "self-help" philosophy working so well. The Bell project proved that her people could accomplish great things independently, without outsiders making decisions for them. But the project benefited Mankiller in a more personal way as well. Through the Bell project, Mankiller formed a strong friendship with her co-organizer, a full-blooded Cherokee named Charlie Lee Soap. Over the years, their friendship deepened, and in 1986, the two married. But this time Mankiller retained her last name.

In the early 1980s, that name grew in importance around the Cherokee Nation headquarters. The Bell project had given Mankiller, as its lead organizer, the chance to have a powerful impact on the fortunes of her tribe. She loved helping her community and continually asked the tribal chief, Ross Swimmer, for more of this kind of work. Her competence and easy authority did not go unnoticed. By 1983, Swimmer had been chief for two terms and was preparing to run for re-election once again. Needing a strong candidate for deputy chief to run with him, Swimmer asked Mankiller to be his running mate.

This invitation took Mankiller, only 38 years old, completely by surprise. The Cherokee Nation at that time consisted of about 75,000 citizens. It had its own congress and constitution, and candidates operated political campaigns just as U.S. politicians do. She had never imagined herself in a high national office, nor in any political office at all for that matter.

Mankiller felt highly honored that Swimmer respected her abilities enough to even suggest this possibility, but stepping into the role of deputy chief seemed out of the question. At first, Mankiller

declined, but then she reconsidered. If she refused this opportunity, how could she ever complain that the Cherokee Nation administration was not doing enough? She went back to Swimmer and accepted the challenge of being his running mate. ᎧᎥ

Ross Swimmer served as chief of the Cherokee Nation for three terms.

Chapter

7 CHIEF OF A NATION

❧

The fight to win the 1983 election had been a difficult one. Mankiller was shocked to find that those who opposed her as deputy chief weren't concerned about her political views on the national level. They were not paying much attention to the platform of ideas she was promoting. The thing they most objected to was that she was a woman.

The idea that a woman should have the responsibility of such a high post was unheard of in the Cherokee Nation. During her campaign, Mankiller was the object of death threats, hate mail, and verbal attacks. But throughout the campaign, she remained poised and her message positive. Despite her foes, all the good she had done within the community had brought her many supporters as well. She had faced

As chief of the Cherokee Nation, Wilma Mankiller met with many important U.S. officials, including President Ronald Reagan.

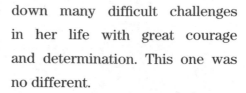
From 1917 until 1971, the U.S. government —specifically the president—took charge of appointing Cherokee chiefs. During these years, the United States refused to recognize nearly all the chiefs democratically elected by the Cherokees themselves. Finally, in 1971, this practice ended and the U.S. government agreed to recognize tribally elected Cherokee chiefs.

down many difficult challenges in her life with great courage and determination. This one was no different.

That determination paid off. Swimmer and Mankiller won the election, and on August 14, 1983, Wilma Mankiller became the first female deputy chief of the Cherokee Nation. In her new role, she supervised more than 40 different Cherokee Nation programs operating in a total of 14 northeastern Oklahoma counties. She administered and advised on programs for daycare and elder care, community building and maintenance projects, education and literacy, and more.

In 1985, Swimmer announced that he would be taking a national position as head of the Bureau of Indian Affairs. The Cherokee Constitution dictated that the deputy chief take over as chief in such a situation. Mankiller would be making history again, this time as the first female chief of the Cherokee Nation.

Mankiller knew that with this great honor came great responsibility. On December 14, 1985, when she was sworn in as the new chief, she felt the pressure

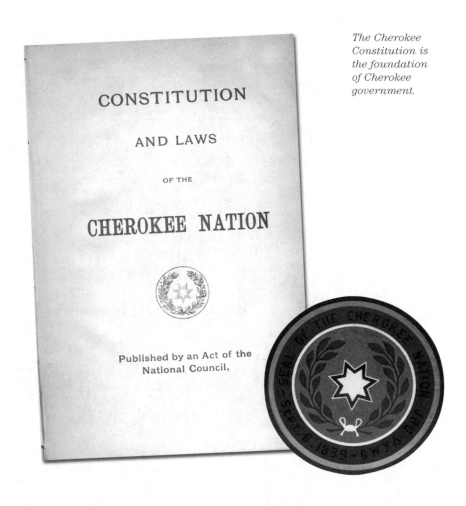

The Cherokee Constitution is the foundation of Cherokee government.

of taking Swimmer's place. She was taking on the role of chief only two years into her four-year term as deputy chief. Furthermore, the Cherokee people had not actually elected her to this highest position of power. Rather, she had inherited the job. She fully expected to meet the same negativity and resistance she had while running for deputy chief. But to her surprise there was no big outcry. Although some of

Wilma Mankiller was 40 years old when she first became chief.

her administration did not wholly support her, she was able to make progress over the next two years. She gained respect in the community and among the council members as well.

By the end of those two years, with election time looming, Mankiller considered entering the race for chief. If she were to win, it would be an undeniable sign that the Cherokee community approved of her as a leader. Mankiller decided to run.

Mankiller's decision to run for chief was

prompted in part by those who doubted she could win. Many, convinced she could never do better than deputy chief, even visited her at home to talk her out of running. But rather than bringing her down, these outside doubters made Mankiller more resolved than ever to rise to the challenge. Once she was chief, she wrote about this experience:

> *I would look out the window and see them coming down the dirt road. ... Finally, I told Charlie that if one more family came down that road and told me not to run, I was going to run for sure. That is just what happened.*

Mankiller had three opponents in the race, and the negative campaigning again swirled around her. But she never lowered herself to respond in the same way. She took the grassroots approach she always had. She visited people in her community and found out what they were thinking and what was bothering them. She took time to get to know them and allow them to learn more about her and what she wanted to bring to the office of chief.

When the 1987 election was held, none of the four candidates for chief received the 50 percent majority needed to win. But with 45 percent of the vote, Mankiller was closest. She and the next-highest contender, a man named

Perry Wheeler, had to compete in a second election. When all the votes from this second election were counted, the winner was clear. Wilma Mankiller had been fairly and unquestionably elected as chief of the Cherokee Nation.

In the summer of 1987, Mankiller was sworn in as chief of the Cherokee Nation for the second time. But for the first time since she had entered politics, taking authority was a joyful experience. When she had taken over from Swimmer in 1985, the people had not directly chosen her. This time she finally had a clear mandate to direct the nation.

Before Mankiller became chief, the U.S. government had traditionally been deeply involved in Cherokee tribal matters, through the Bureau of Indian Affairs (BIA). But in 1990, she achieved a historic milestone in tribal self-governance. She signed an agreement with the BIA that gave the Cherokees and five other tribes full responsibility for overseeing the use of $6.1 million in funds. Up until that point, the BIA had been exclusively in charge of how this money would be spent.

Mankiller defined the role of the Cherokee Nation administration as being, more than anything else, a resource for the people. Her concept of how the central government should function was different from that of most other Native American governments. She believed the best way for her people to gain self-respect and pride was to put each Cherokee community in charge of its own change. Under her administration, each individual community would take responsibility for planning, building, and maintaining projects that would improve the lives of its people. These communities would look to the central government as a facilitator in successfully accomplishing the projects and improvements they determined for themselves. These projects would include things like developing waterworks, building schools and clinics, and much more.

Mankiller's administration helped bring new and modern schools to the Cherokee Nation.

Getting tribal communities to begin taking the lead in making a difference in the quality of life was

In 1989, Mankiller met with Choctaw Chief Philip Martin.

a difficult task. The idea was virtually unheard-of among other Native American tribes. But Mankiller had always had deep faith in this approach. Over the four years of her first full term as chief, changes started to occur at every level. New energy infused the nation as Cherokees began to demonstrate their vast ability to do what needed to be done. Over and over, they proved they could make their own lives better if given the opportunity.

In 1991, Cherokee Nation elections came again. This time, Mankiller felt no hesitation in putting in her bid for reelection as chief. During the six years she had already spent in office, she had made a major impact on the way the Cherokee people viewed themselves and what they saw themselves capable of. The Cherokee Nation had truly been revitalized. But there was much work still to be done. Mankiller wanted to be the one to continue to guide that process.

Once again, election results showed that her people agreed she was the one for the job. In a stunning victory, Mankiller captured 82.7 percent of the vote. On August 14, 1991, she began her second full term as chief.

> *Many of the community development programs Mankiller helped create through the Cherokee Nation relied on the ideas, knowledge, and labor of tribe members themselves. Mankiller said that her experiences in California and Oklahoma had taught her that "poor people have a much, much greater capacity for solving their own problems than most people give them credit for."*

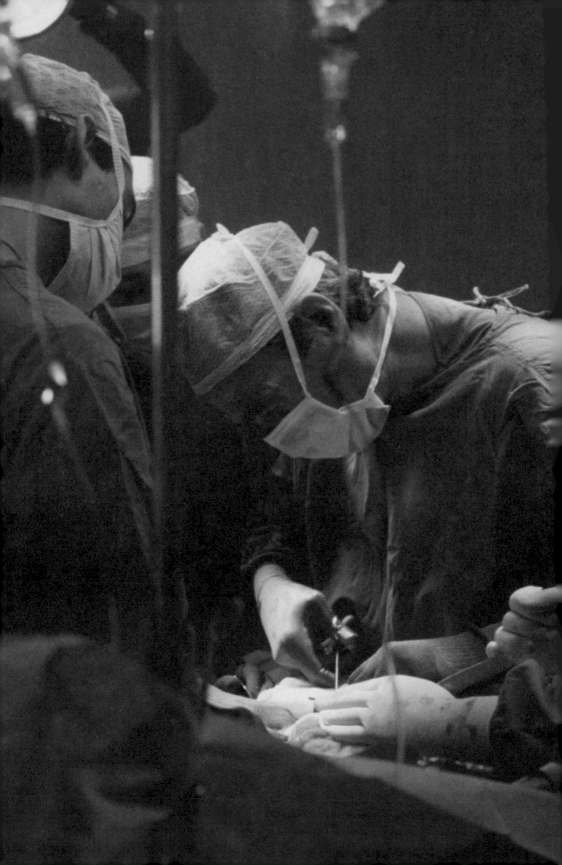

8 Chapter
TRIALS OF THE BODY

ை✕ை

By 1991, Wilma Mankiller could count many great triumphs on the professional level. Behind the scenes, however, she was continuously plagued with physical problems. Back in 1964, while pregnant with her first daughter, Mankiller had suffered a bad kidney infection. Shortly after the death of her father in 1971, these infections began to recur. Tests to discover the problem had not brought good news. Mankiller was stunned to learn that she had the same kidney disease from which her father had died.

The doctors had explained to Mankiller that over time her kidneys would become increasingly diseased until she suffered complete kidney failure. Mankiller had tried to remain optimistic that her kidneys would not completely fail as her father's

A kidney transplant is a two-part operation: one part to remove the healthy kidney from the donor and another part to insert the new kidney into the patient.

had. She tried numerous treatments and surgical procedures. But her condition continued to worsen, and in 1987, shortly before her first election as chief, Mankiller was hospitalized with a long and severe kidney infection. Unfortunately, while in the hospital her condition had been misdiagnosed. This had led to massive kidney damage that could not be reversed. To survive, she would ultimately need a kidney transplant.

In June 1990, well into her first full term as chief, Mankiller underwent the three-hour transplant surgery in Boston. Her eldest brother, Don, who had no trace of the disease, generously acted as her kidney donor.

With a new, well-functioning kidney, Mankiller resumed the duties of her office in August 1990. She continued working as hard as she ever had through the rest of that term and into her next. Her strong vision of a revitalized nation continued to guide her as leader throughout her successful second full term, from 1991 through 1995.

Many people who have suffered kidney damage are kept alive by a process called dialysis. A tube connects a machine to an artery in the patient's arm. Blood flows through the machine, which removes wastes, and then back into the arm. Patients generally undergo dialysis for several hours, three times a week. Other patients have a kidney transplant. The replacement kidney usually comes from a close relative in order for the organ to best match the patient's tissues. But most other replacement organs come from unrelated donors who have died in accidents or from other causes.

But as the 1995 elections loomed, Mankiller began to think deeply about what she wanted for her future. She was torn. Many wanted her to run for chief a third time, and she herself found it hard to imagine not continuing in office. Including her terms as both deputy chief and chief, Mankiller had served the Cherokee Nation a total of 12 years.

And she had done the job with widely acknowledged excellence. Under her leadership, the Cherokee tribe had doubled its membership. By 1991, the nation boasted 108,000 citizens, making it only second in size to the Navajo Nation and the largest nonreservation tribe in the United States. Additionally, the tribal budget had increased to $90 million, nearly twice as large as before Mankiller took office.

Mankiller had presided over the development of an active Job Corps designed to help Cherokee teens acquire the skills they would need for decent employment. Business and industry advancements made during her terms in office were providing

Mankiller's groundbreaking role as first female chief set the stage for many other Native American women to enter into tribal politics. Several have since won political races, both in the Cherokee Nation as well as in other tribes. A few have even been elected chief, or president, of their tribe. One of these is Cecelia Fire Thunder, who took office in December 2004 as the first female leader of the Oglala Sioux, a tribe that has had such famous leaders as Red Cloud and Crazy Horse.

economic aid to many areas of the Cherokee Nation.
Under her watch, infant mortality and unemployment
were declining, and she had overseen the establish-
ment of cultural programs and health clinics, as well
as the important Institute for Cherokee Literacy.
The cycle of poverty had been broken for many of her
citizens, and deeply ingrained negative stereotypes of
Native American people were beginning to dissolve.

*Wilma
Mankiller and
other Native
American
leaders met
with President
Bill Clinton
to discuss
tribal issues.*

During her tenure, Mankiller herself had become
a nationally recognized political and spiritual force, as
well as a risk-taking social reformer. She had testified
before Congress about Indian rights and sovereignty.

In 1986, she had been named the American Indian Woman of the Year. The following year, she was named Woman of the Year by the feminist publication *Ms.* magazine. Still, despite her many successes, the work and education yet to be done were limitless.

After giving the matter long thought and discussing the advantages and disadvantages with friends, family, and especially with her husband, Mankiller made the difficult decision. She would not run for chief in 1995. A new phase of her life was about to begin.

Though Mankiller had withdrawn from political life, she was still concerned about many issues, such as minority education and the negative stereotypes of Native Americans. She vowed to continue championing the causes she had focused on in office.

The year 1996 began on a positive note. After stepping down from office, Mankiller accepted a Montgomery Fellowship at Dartmouth College in Hanover, New Hampshire, beginning in January

Through the honor of being named Ms. magazine's Woman of the Year in 1987, Mankiller became good friends with Gloria Steinem, a famous feminist and the magazine's editor-in-chief. When Steinem got married in 2000, she did so at Mankiller Flats. The ceremony, which was done in part according to Cherokee tradition, was jointly performed by a local judge and Mankiller's husband, Charlie Soap, who is trained in Cherokee spiritual tradition.

New Hampshire's Dartmouth College was founded in 1769.

1996. She would lecture, take part in seminars, and be able to do much reading, writing, and research in a supportive academic environment.

The only downside of this decision was that Mankiller's husband, Charlie, could not accompany her to the East Coast. Charlie had three sons from former marriages. The two youngest, Cobey and Winterhawk, were still in school in Oklahoma. He needed to stay at home with them.

Without Charlie there, Mankiller was alone and far from Mankiller Flats when pneumonia struck her that winter. She had had colds and other mild physical problems since arriving in Hanover, but expected nothing unusual when she went to be treated for the pneumonia. Instead, she received more distressing news. After all she had been through already, Mankiller had another grave challenge to face. Tests revealed she had lymphoma, a form of cancer.

Devastated by this new attack on her body, Mankiller withdrew from her fellowship in late February, a week before it ended. As she said goodbye to Dartmouth, she did not realize that she would be spending the coming 28 months again battling for her life.

For five weeks in early 1996, Mankiller lay in a Boston hospital. Charlie, other family, and close friends were there to support her, while doctors ran tests and tried to determine the best course of treatment for her. Since her body was already weakened from her kidney transplant, doctors feared traditional cancer treatments might actually prove harmful. So during her long weeks in the hospital, Mankiller explored many different kinds of alternative treatments. She used Native

Cancer is a disease in which cells multiply wildly, destroy healthy tissue, and endanger life. About 100 kinds of cancer attack people. Lymphoma is a cancer of the lymphatic system, a network of vessels that returns fluids to the bloodstream and helps fight disease. It is most often treated through surgery, radiation therapy, or drug therapy (chemotherapy).

American herbal remedies, changed her diet, and practiced meditation.

But in time, it became clear that she needed something stronger. Finally, with her doctors' agreement, Mankiller decided to try a regimen of chemotherapy, which would be followed by radiation treatment.

After completing chemotherapy treatments in August 1996, Mankiller returned home to Oklahoma in the fall to begin radiation. But for all the good these methods did in fighting her cancer, her kidney was now failing rapidly. She began receiving regular dialysis to keep the vital organ functioning, but this led to other problems.

As the determined fighter she had always been, Mankiller braved these assaults on her body. She also remained deeply involved in tribal and community activities. While undergoing treatment, she managed to do fund raising for various important causes, helped her husband build a Boys and Girls Club in Tahlequah, and co-edited a book with her friend Gloria Steinem on American women's history. But her failing health was always at the front of her mind. Throughout 1997, she tried further alternative treatments and endured many blood transfusions. Finally, in early 1998, she was able to declare a significant victory: She had beaten the lymphoma. There was no cancer remaining in her body.

Her kidney, however, continued to fail. Without another transplant operation, Mankiller again faced imminent death. This time, the precious kidney was supplied by Mankiller's niece, 32-year-old Virlee Williamson. The transplant took place in July 1998 and was completely successful. Mankiller's body accepted the new kidney, and it worked properly from the start. Like a cat with nine lives, Mankiller had once again been spared. ❧

While undergoing cancer and kidney treatments, Mankiller spoke at a women's benefit, along with Angela Y. Davis (left) and Gloria Steinem.

9 Chapter

A Phoenix Rising

❧⌘❧

A cat is said to have nine lives. But there is another powerful symbol of rebirth and renewal from the animal kingdom, too. This is the symbol of the phoenix, a legendary bird that rises again from the ashes after being consumed by fire.

This mythical creature is well-known to the Cherokee people. With the push west of the whites in the 1800s, the Cherokee culture nearly went down in flames itself. Today, the Cherokee Nation is again strong and vital, rising from the ashes of a difficult past. This is due in large part to the efforts of Wilma Mankiller.

Mankiller might be considered something of a phoenix, too. She has risen out of adversity time and again, surviving intense challenges, both personal

Wilma Mankiller continues to be active as a speaker, teacher, writer, and activist.

and political. Throughout the most severe physical trials she has prevailed. With another new kidney came new life. And with the turn of the century, Mankiller remains a strong and vibrant leader in Native American issues. She is continually recognized for her invaluable contributions to both Cherokee life and culture, and the world at large.

In 1998, Mankiller was awarded the Presidential Medal of Freedom by President Bill Clinton. This is the highest honor awarded to a civilian by the U.S. government. It recognizes individuals who have made "an especially meritorious contribution to the security or national interests of the United States, or to world peace, or to cultural or other significant public or private endeavors." She has received a Citation for Outstanding Contributions to American Leadership and Native American Culture from the Harvard Foundation (1986). She has also been inducted into the Oklahoma Women's Hall of Fame (1986), Governor's Advisory Committee (1986), and the National Women's Hall of Fame (1993). Mankiller, who was the first in her family

Wilma Mankiller's honors and awards continue to accumulate. But one that stands out as most special to her was a seemingly small gesture. It occurred at a memorial service being presided over by several male tribal elders and clearly indicated the high standing she had achieved among the Cherokees. The men invited her to sit with them in an area designated only for respected elders.

to attend and graduate from college, has also been awarded honorary doctorate degrees from Oklahoma State University, Yale University, and numerous other institutions.

President Bill Clinton awarded Wilma Mankiller with the Presidential Medal of Freedom.

In the spring of 2005, Mankiller was publicly announced as the Morse Chair professor for the fall 2005 semester at the University of Oregon in Eugene. She was selected because of her renown as an activist, her knowledge of legal policy, and her work with Native American tribes. Mankiller accepted the appointment as an opportunity to further causes close to her heart. Topping this list are bringing a broader awareness of contemporary Native American issues, giving such issues a historical context, and casting greater light on Native American stereotypes in order to dissolve them. Her primary duties as professor were public lectures and co-teaching of an ethnic studies class titled "Native American Life, Law, and Leadership" to upper-division students.

Since the time she was a young woman, Mankiller has devoted her life to the service of others. She continues to travel frequently for speaking engagements, to join in panels, and to promote the causes she so deeply believes in. Still, Mankiller finds time to pursue more personal interests as well. She enjoys spending time with family. Her daughters both married men with Cherokee ancestry, and both now have children of their own.

Some of her most enjoyable and relaxing time is spent cooking. She likes to organize groups of women to cook together for tribal events and benefits. In a cookbook she published in 1988, *The Chief Cooks:*

In 1997, Mankiller spoke before a commission about the Cherokee Nation.

Traditional Cherokee Recipes, Mankiller wrote:

> *I appreciate good food and the nurturing it represents. I know also that cooking brings the happiness and warmth synonymous with home and family so important in Cherokee culture.*

Since that time, Mankiller has published other

One of Mankiller's favorite Cherokee recipes is easy to make. Put four cups of chicken broth, four cups of milk, and four cups of water together in a big pot. Add a pound of very finely ground roasted peanuts. Grind about a quarter of the nuts longer than the rest—until you have a thick paste. Add all the nuts to the pot and stir the mixture frequently as it simmers. In about 30 minutes, you've got delicious peanut soup!

books celebrating and educating the public about that which she holds most dear—the cultures of the Cherokee and other indigenous tribes. In 1993, her autobiography, titled *Mankiller: A Chief and Her People*, was released. Her latest book, titled *Every Day Is a Good Day: Reflections of Contemporary Indigenous Women*, was published in 2004.

Mankiller's work and her writings have gone a long way toward establishing respect for Native American culture and building respect for the Cherokee Nation in particular. As she wrote about native cultures in her book *Every Day is a Good Day*, "It is almost impossible for an outsider to grasp the underlying values of the community or the culture and lifeways of the people and their relationship to the natural world."

Like her ancestors who walked the Trail of Tears nearly 170 years ago, Mankiller was torn from that natural world as a child. But the power of the land has remained a major influence in her life. Like those ancestors, she is a survivor. She has survived to pass along greater understanding of her people and their

history to all those who might not have otherwise understood. For this and so many other reasons, Wilma Mankiller will long be known not simply as the first female leader of her nation. She will go down in history as one of the most exceptional and revered of all Cherokee chiefs. ❧

Mankiller's influence on the Cherokee Nation cannot be underestimated.

MANKILLER'S LIFE

1945

Born November 18 in
Tahlequah, Oklahoma

1956

Relocates with
family to
San Francisco,
California

1963

Marries Hector Hugo
Olaya de Bardi in
November

1945

1960

1945

World War II
(1939–1945) ends

1961

The Berlin Wall is
built, dividing East
and West Germany

WORLD EVENTS

1969–1971

Works as an activist during the Native American takeover of Alcatraz Island

1977

Moves back to Mankiller Flats, Oklahoma, and begins working for the Cherokee Nation

1970

1966

The National Organization for Women (NOW) is established to work for equality between women and men

1969

U.S. astronauts are the first humans to land on the moon

1976

U.S. military academies admit women

MANKILLER'S LIFE

1979

Suffers a near-fatal automobile accident on November 9

1981

Helps to found the Cherokee Nation Community Development Department

1983

Elected deputy chief of the Cherokee Nation

1980

1978

The first test-tube baby conceived outside its mother's womb is born in Oldham, England

1981

Sandra Day O'Connor becomes the first woman on the U.S. Supreme Court

1983

The AIDS (acquired immune deficiency syndrome) virus is identified

WORLD EVENTS

1985
Succeeds Ross Swimmer as chief of the Cherokee Nation

1986
Marries second husband, Charlie Soap

1987
Elected first female chief of the Cherokee Nation

1985

1985
Associated Press newsman Terry Anderson is taken hostage in Beirut, Lebanon; he would be released in December 1991

1986
The U.S. space shuttle Challenger explodes, killing all seven astronauts on board

1987
Stock markets fall sharply around the world on Black Monday, October 19

MANKILLER'S LIFE

1990

Undergoes kidney transplant in June

1991

Elected chief of Cherokee Nation for second term

1995

Retires from public office and accepts a fellowship at Dartmouth University

1990

1990

Political prisoner Nelson Mandela, a leader of the anti-apartheid movement in South Africa, is released; Mandela becomes president of South Africa in 1994

1994

Genocide of 500,000 to 1 million of the minority Tutsi group by rival Hutu people in Rwanda

WORLD EVENTS

1996
Diagnosed with
cancer and returns
to Mankiller Flats

1998
Defeats cancer but
undergoes a second
kidney transplant

1999—PRESENT
Continues work as
a Native American
rights activist and
becomes an author,
public lecturer, and
university professor

1996
A sheep is cloned
in Scotland

2005
Major earthquake
kills thousands in
Pakistan

2001
Terrorist attacks on
two World Trade Center
Towers in New York City
and on the Pentagon in
Washington, D.C., leave
thousands dead

DATE OF BIRTH: November 18, 1945

BIRTHPLACE: Tahlequah, Oklahoma

FATHER: Charley Mankiller (1914–1971)

MOTHER: Clara Irene Sitton Mankiller (1921–)

EDUCATION: Skyline Junior College; San Francisco State University; University of Arkansas

FIRST SPOUSE: Hector Hugo Olaya de Bardi

DATE OF MARRIAGE: November 13, 1963

CHILDREN: Felicia (1964–) Gina (1966–)

SECOND SPOUSE: Charlie Lee Soap

DATE OF MARRIAGE: October 1986

FURTHER READING

Kallen, Stuart A. *Native American Chiefs and Warriors.* San Diego, Calif.: Lucent Books, 1999.

Lazo, Caroline Evensen. *Wilma Mankiller.* New York: Dillon Press, 1994.

Schwarz, Melissa. *Wilma Mankiller: Principal Chief of the Cherokees.* New York: Chelsea House, 1994.

Yannuzzi, Della A. *Wilma Mankiller: Leader of the Cherokee Nation.* Hillside, N.J.: Enslow Publishers, 1994.

LOOK FOR MORE SIGNATURE LIVES
BOOKS ABOUT THIS ERA:

Andrew Carnegie: *Captain of Industry*
ISBN 0-7565-0995-5

Carrie Chapman Catt: *A Voice for Women*
ISBN 0-7565-0991

Henry B. Gonzalez: *Congressman of the People*
ISBN 0-7565-0996-3

J. Edgar Hoover: *Controversial FBI Director*
ISBN 0-7565-0997-1

Langston Hughes: *The Voice of Harlem*
ISBN 0-7565-0993-9

Douglas MacArthur: *America's General*
ISBN 0-7565-0994-7

Eleanor Roosevelt: *First Lady of the World*
ISBN 0-7565-0992-0

Franklin Roosevelt: *The New Deal President*
ISBN 0-7565-1586-6

Elizabeth Cady Stanton: *Social Reformer*
ISBN 0-7565-0990-4

Gloria Steinem: *Champion of Womens Rights*
ISBN 0-7565-1587-4

On the Web

For more information on *Wilma Mankiller*, use FactHound.

1. Go to *www.facthound.com*
2. Type in a search word related to this book or this book ID: 0756516005
3. Click on the *Fetch It* button.

FactHound will fetch the best Web sites for you.

Historic Sites

Cherokee Heritage Center
21192 Keeler
Park Hill, OK 74451
918/456-6007
Two reconstructed Cherokee villages, a Trail of Tears exhibit, art galleries, and a 4,000-volume library

New Echota—First Capital of the Cherokee Nation
1211 Chatsworth Highway N.E.
Calhoun, GA 30701
706/624-1321
Historic town containing the Cherokee Supreme Court building, historic Cherokee homes, and a museum of Cherokee history

arson
setting a fire for the purpose of doing harm

bureaucratic
a way of doing things characterized by time-consuming effort and complications

chemotherapy
the use of drugs or chemicals to combat disease

clan
a group of people related by a common ancestor

dialysis
a process that uses a machine to remove waste from the blood, a process usually performed by the human kidneys

evicted
forced out

facilitator
one who helps something to happen

feminist
someone who believes strongly that women ought to have the same opportunities and rights as men have

foreboding
a feeling that something bad is about to occur

grassroots
dealing at the most fundamental, person-to-person level

homestead
to acquire and settle on a piece of land

idyllic
picturesque, simple, and natural

Glossary

indigenous
originating in a particular environment or geographical region

inducted
admitted as a member

literacy
the ability to read and write

mandate
authorization for a leader to take command due to widespread public favor

muscular dystrophy
a chronic disease of the muscles that causes varying degrees of weakness in the voluntary muscles of the body

shaman
a religious leader and healer of a tribe

syllabary
a series or set of written characters in which each character is used to represent a syllable

tenure
term in office

Chapter 1

Page 10, line 5: Wilma Mankiller and Michael Wallis. *Mankiller: A Chief and Her People.* New York: St. Martin's Press, 1993, p. 14.

Chapter 2

Page 23, line 12: Ibid., p 32.

Page 26, sidebar: Ibid., p. 77.

Chapter 3

Page 37, sidebar: Ibid., p. 83.

Chapter 4

Page 43, line 14: Ibid., p. 159.

Chapter 5

Page 52, line 14: Ibid., p. 205.

Chapter 6

Page 62, line 2: Ibid., pp. 223–224.

Page 63, sidebar: Ibid., p. 226.

Chapter 7

Page 73, line 8: Ibid., p. 247.

Page 77, sidebar: Wilma Mankiller. "Rebuilding the Cherokee Nation." Sweet Briar College. April 2, 1993. *Gifts of Speech.* 30 Nov. 2005. http://gos.sbc.edu/m/mankiller.html

Chapter 9

Page 90, line 12: *Code of Federal Regulations.* Title 32, Section 578.4.

Page 93, line 2: Beverly Cox and Martin Jacobs. "Mankiller Cooking: The Chief Chef." *Native Peoples.* Sept./Oct. 2003, p. 22.

Page 94, line 19: Wilma Mankiller. *Every Day Is a Good Day: Reflections of Contemporary Indigenous Women.* Golden, Colo.: Fulcrum Publishing, 2004, p. 30.

Adcock, Clifton. "Mankiller Helped Lead the Way in Oklahoma." *Muskogee Daily Phoenix and Times-Democrat* (OK). November 27, 2004.

"Alcatraz is Not an Island." Indian Activism/PBS Web site. <http://www.pbs.org/itvs/alcatrazisnotanisland/activism.html> 12 April 2005.

Carter III, Samuel. *Cherokee Sunset: A Nation Betrayed.* Garden City, N.Y.: Doubleday & Co., Inc., 1976.

Cox, Beverly, and Martin Jacobs. "Mankiller Cooking: The Chief Chef." *Native Peoples.* Sept./Oct. 2003.

Ehle, John. *Trail of Tears: The Rise and Fall of the Cherokee Nation.* New York: Doubleday, 1988.

Fischer, Kent. "Lessons in Tolerance: Former Cherokee Chief Brings Experience to Dartmouth." *Black Issues in Higher Education.* Jan. 25, 1996.

Gilbert, Joan. *The Trail of Tears Across Missouri.* Columbia: University of Missouri Press, 1996.

Kilpatrick, Alan. *The Night Has a Naked Soul: Witchcraft and Sorcery Among the Western Cherokee.* Syracuse, N.Y.: Syracuse University Press, 1998.

Mankiller, Wilma. "Education and Native Americans: Entering the Twenty-First Century on Our Own Terms." *National Forum.* Spring, 1991.

Mankiller, Wilma. *Every Day Is a Good Day: Reflections of Contemporary Indigenous Women.* Golden, Colo.: Fulcrum Publishing, 2004.

Mankiller, Wilma, and Michael Wallis. *Mankiller: A Chief and Her People.* New York: St. Martin's Griffin, 1993.

Mankiller, Wilma. "People Expect Me to be More Warlike." *U.S. News & World Report.* Feb. 17, 1986.

Waldman, Carl. *Atlas of the North American Indian.* New York: Checkmark Books, 2000.

Waldrop, Judith. "Mankiller's Challenge." *American Demographics.* June 1987.

Woster, Terry. "More Women Buck Tradition, Take Reins of Indian Tribes." *Muskogee Daily Phoenix and Times-Democrat* (OK). November 27, 2004.

Pamela Dell began her professional career writing for adults and started writing for children about 12 years ago. Since then she has published fiction and nonfiction books, written numerous magazine articles, and created award-winning interactive multimedia.

Image Credits

TURNING OFF THE MORNING NEWS

Scene 1

A living room. Probably not a full kind of set, but just something that suggests a living room.

Jimmy enters. He is mid-40s probably. He seems troubled. He is maybe in jeans and plaid shirt or a dark shirt. Definitely not in a suit. He addresses the audience.

JIMMY. I am feeling very depressed. I'm thinking of killing myself. Or maybe going to a nearby mall and killing other people, and then killing myself. Maybe I'll go to a theater and kill people there and then kill myself. You're lucky I'm in the play, and not in the audience. Talk to you again later.

He goes back to where he came from—which is the kitchen.

A bit of a pause. His wife, Polly, comes out from the same place. She is carrying a rather large potted plant. She speaks to the audience.

POLLY. Hello. I'm sorry about the wallpaper. My husband wouldn't let me change it. Do you like this plant? It needs water, I keep meaning to put water in it, but I'm not in the kitchen and there's not a sink here. So I'll have to try to remember when I get back to the kitchen to put water in this plant. Plus it's heavy. I'm going to put it down for a while.

She puts the plant on the ground.

Have you seen my husband? I thought I heard him speaking to you. He's such a sweet man. He's really lovely. But he's very sensitive, and thinks he's useless. Which is too bad. I tell him I think he's wonderful, but he thinks I'm stupid and I think everyone is wonderful. And

5

everyone is wonderful, don't you think so. Or even if they're not, you should tell them they're wonderful. My husband hasn't spoken to me for about three weeks. But then I talk so much he often screams at me to be quiet, but it's hard for me to be quiet.

I mean that's how God created Eve, she was very talkative and had a long discussion with the Serpent, and the Serpent realized Eve was chatty, and he talked and talked to her about all the knowledge she'd get if she ate from the apple, and how many more topics she could talk about in her conversations, and lo and behold once she ate part of the apple and then had her husband Adam eat the rest of the apple, well then, Eve created sickness, death, divorce, and murder at the local malls. And it's because God made Eve so chatty. It's really not my fault. Or rather it's her fault.

But I need to talk because I find life so overwhelming, I don't quite know how to live on the earth. I mean I've been in three car accidents, my husband was driving all three times, two times he drove off a bridge into a big river, but our windows were open both times, so we were able to swim out of the car. I'm a very good swimmer, I could have gone to the Olympics but I could never find the address of how to apply. And so my life hasn't amounted to too much, but I'm not bitter. I love God even though he made me chatty and had me be the one—or my ancestors—who caused death and sickness. But I think sickness makes you stronger. Or makes you dead. But then you go to heaven. And heaven, oh how I long to get to heaven. No sickness and death, and I get to talk as much as I want to.

Where is the potted plant do you know?

It's right in front of her.

I can't see it. Do you know where I put it? Maybe it's in the kitchen. I'll be back.

She goes off to the kitchen.

(Offstage.) Hello, darling. How are you today?

The sound of gunshots. She screams a lot. Comes back in.

Thank God he's a bad shot. *(Calls offstage.)* Please don't shoot your gun at me that way, it makes me upset. Have you taken your herbal thing for depression? Jimmy? Jimmy?

(Singing suddenly, to herself.) "Jimmy crack corn and I don't care, Jimmy crack corn and I don't care."

(Calls offstage.) I don't care, Jimmy. I want you to act more normal, okay? Promise?

(To audience.) Really he's a lovely guy. He has his ups and downs, but everyone does, don't you think.

Oh look, *there's* the potted plant. Why didn't you tell me where it was? You're not very helpful. I have a difficult life, and you could at least try to help.

> *Enter Timmy, her 13-year-old son. He is played by someone 16–23 who looks young. He is sensitive and shy. He is coming into the house from outside. Maybe he carries a book bag from school.*

Oh here's Timmy, my son. He's in the eighth grade. He's very shy. Aren't you, Timmy? I know he looks 17 or 18, but we didn't want to cast a real 13-year-old. Or maybe he IS 13, and he just looks older.

How was school today, Timmy? Did you make any friends today?

> *He shakes his head no.*

Oh too bad. Did you try? I just go up to people and I say, I'm Polly, what's your name? Want to be my friend? Did you try that today?

TIMMY. Yes I said "My name is Polly" and then they all laughed at me.

POLLY. No, dear, Polly is *my* name, I meant for you to use YOUR name. Polly is a girl's name.

TIMMY. I know. Everyone said he's a girl, he's a girl.

POLLY. Well it's sort of your fault, you said your name was Polly.

TIMMY. I got scared.

POLLY. All right, dear. You're just not very smart. *(Changes her response.)* I'm sorry. You're very smart. And you're Mommy's little girl. I mean boy. Oh God. Why can't I be a swimmer in the Olympics?

> *Enter Jimmy.*

Oh you don't have your gun. Good. Did you lock it up so you can't get it?

JIMMY. I'm depressed.

POLLY. Have you taken your St. John's wort today?

JIMMY. I can't find it.

POLLY. Oh you're as bad as me with the potted plant.

JIMMY. I can either kill you and Timmy, and then myself. Or I can go to the mall and shoot strangers and then kill myself.

POLLY. Darling, don't do either. Just take a nap or something. Tomorrow is another day.

JIMMY. Make up your mind. You and Timmy, or strangers at the mall. Make up your mind.

POLLY. Neither.

JIMMY. WHICH ONE, WHICH ONE???

POLLY. Okay people at the mall!

JIMMY. Okay.

> *Jimmy exits back into the kitchen.*

TIMMY. I'm scared.

POLLY. Well life is scary, what can I say?

> *Jimmy comes back in. He is carrying two big assault rifles and multiple bullets around his waist. He is also wearing a pig head mask.* *

Oh, Timmy's Halloween mask. Are you feeling playful, darling?

JIMMY. Goodbye. You'll never see me again. And don't forget, you're the one who said go to the mall. You have ruined my life. Timmy's too. I could have been a famous author on Amazon. Or I could have been a senator or a governor or a clown in the circus.

> *Jimmy starts to put his two guns inside a big black garbage bag.*

But everything I wanted to do, you ruined. Life has not been fair to me.

POLLY. Oh! *(Noticing the garbage bag.)* Are you throwing out your guns, I hope?

---

* Note: I did "Google Image" for Halloween hat that covers head, and saw a very funny, non-scary pig head.

JIMMY. That's a stupid question. No, I'm just covering them up until I get there.

POLLY. Get where?

JIMMY. I deserved better! I deserved better!

He exits in a fury. Timmy seems very scared. Polly takes it in stride.

POLLY. Well your father is so unpredictable. I didn't know he wanted to write books, did you?

TIMMY. Shouldn't we call the police?

POLLY. You have to have an impulse to be a writer. You can't just say "I'm a writer" all of a sudden. Your father is so impractical. On the other hand, he's just super sensitive, we have to be patient.

TIMMY. Shouldn't we call the police?

POLLY. Goodness, why?

TIMMY. Well he's going to kill people at the mall.

POLLY. Darling, he had a Halloween mask on. So he's playing with us. If he was serious he wouldn't put such a silly thing on his head. Your father is many things, he's bipolar, he's a depressive, he sometimes ties me to the bed and drips candle wax on my body—I'm sorry, I shouldn't have told you that. Forget I said it.

TIMMY. How can I forget it?

POLLY. *(Very annoyed.)* Well, try to, darling, alright? Gosh, give your mother a little slack. Anyway my point is that your father isn't going to kill people, he knows better than that. So I don't want to involve the police in this. They have enough to do with people speeding and so on. You know I'm worried how you're doing in school. And you don't make friends, and I have a hundred friends. All of them named Mary. But you don't have any friends. Are you learning anything in school? I think I should homeschool you so you can get proper morals as well as accurate information about the world.

TIMMY. No, I don't want you to be my teacher. I need some outside opinions from other people. And what do you mean you have a hundred friends named Mary? I can only think of one.

POLLY. All right, well subtract ninety-nine from one hundred, and you get one. I have one friend named Mary. That was fun, the subtracting thing. I have a feeling homeschooling is in your future, buddy boy.

TIMMY. *(At random.)* Help! Help!

POLLY. *(As if it's funny, lighthearted.)* Oh you! Shut up. *(To herself.)* Now where is that potted plant? I need to water it.

> *Polly looks around, it's right in front of her, but she just doesn't see it. Timmy looks at her in despair.*
>
> *Lights dim.*

Scene 2

> *The neighbors' house next door. Clifford is in the living room, listening to classical music. He addresses the audience.*

CLIFFORD. I find classical music soothing in the morning. Or any time. I used to start with the news. Remember when Katie Couric was on the news. She was very relaxing and friendly. But now on ABC they're always laughing their heads off about something, all six of them in a row laughing. And then of course they don't laugh when something terrible happens, which is more and more frequent.

> *Somehow he looks out the window.*

Oh excuse me for a second. Something odd is out the window.

> *He goes closer to the window.*

Huh. Hmmm. Disturbing.

> *He aims a remote in front of him to turn off the music; calls:*

Salena! Come look at this.

> *Enter Salena, a vibrant black woman, late 30s. She's attractive and energetic.*

SALENA. Look at what?

CLIFFORD. Oh. You just missed him. He just left. It was kind of weird.

SALENA. What was weird? What are you talking about?

CLIFFORD. It's that guy next door. Remember, I told you I tried to introduce myself a couple days ago, and he kind of ran to his car.

SALENA. Uh-huh.

CLIFFORD. Well he just left the house, and he had this big pig head he was wearing.

SALENA. Pig head. Huh. Was it a scary pig head?

CLIFFORD. Well not exactly. Maybe it's scary he was wearing it. And he drove away in the car. Why would he have it on his head?

SALENA. Maybe he needs to avoid the sun. The sun rays are stronger than they used to be, Rosalind was telling me. That woman I met. She's had twenty-four basal cells on her face and neck, and now she only goes out if she's wearing a pillowcase on her head, with little holes for her eyes and nose.

CLIFFORD. Pillowcase. Why doesn't she just put on sunscreen?

SALENA. Well, she wears glasses, and the sunscreen gets in her eyes. Also you have to keep putting sunscreen on every few hours, and so she finds it easier to just wear a pillowcase.

CLIFFORD. I see. But why was the neighbor wearing a pig's head?

SALENA. I don't know. Why don't you ring the bell and ask his wife?

CLIFFORD. No. I think that would be a bad way to introduce ourselves as the new neighbors. I mean maybe it's a joke at his office or something.

SALENA. Oh he works at an office?

CLIFFORD. Well I don't know. Yesterday I said "hello, I'm your new neighbor," and he said something I couldn't hear, and then he ran to his car and drove away. And now I just saw him getting into his car wearing this... pig's head.

SALENA. You're sounding like James Stewart in *Rear Window*— you know, when he's constantly looking out his window all the time, seeing what people are doing inside their apartments. And then he thinks he's seen something bad.

CLIFFORD. Well I'm not using binoculars like he did. Plus he was right, something *was* wrong in one of the apartments. I mean—it isn't Halloween. I can't figure out if it's a joke, or if it's something malevolent.

SALENA. Well Rosalind has been living here for a while, maybe I should ask her about the people next door.

CLIFFORD. *(Admiring.)* You're so much better at meeting people than I am. How did you meet Rosalind?

SALENA. Well no one has been knocking on our doors since we got here, so I had an idea how to meet people, and so I went to the schoolbus stop near us, and I stood with all the mothers and their children.

CLIFFORD. You did? Didn't they look at you funny standing there with no child?

SALENA. Well yes people looked at me a bit funny. And there were no other black people at the bus stop, and I had this impulse to say "Does anyone want me to do your laundry?" But then I thought they might not take it as a joke; so I couldn't figure out how to start a conversation when Rosalind came to the bus stop, and she was friendly immediately. And said she thought she lived right across the street from us. And were we the couple who moved in two weeks ago?

CLIFFORD. *(Not a big deal, he just wants clarity.)* She said couple? Did you explain we're not husband and wife, but just living together because we…sort of had similar misfortunes.

SALENA. Well mine was a lot less than yours. Besides Rosalind talks a lot and is hard to interrupt. She's a big presence, and she was wearing this pillowcase on her head and her son was holding an umbrella over *his* head even though it wasn't raining. And I was about to ask her about the pillowcase and the umbrella, but she just blurted out in a friendly way that she had had all these basal cells on her face and neck, and she was just avoiding the sun as much as she possibly could. But then the bus came. And while the children were getting on the bus, one of them said to one of the other boys, "How are you today, Polly?" And then several other children started to chant "Polly Polly Polly," including Rosalind's son, although Rosalind said "stop that and his name is Timmy, and leave him alone." And then the bus drove away, and Rosalind said children are so mean sometimes, how did we ever grow up?

And then she said, Goodness, did your child get on the bus, I didn't see him if he did. And I said I don't have any children. And she said, well I don't know why you're here then, but you don't look like a kidnapper, so let's have coffee sometime soon, but right now I have to go see my dermatologist. And then she walked away. But I think she's going to be a friend.

CLIFFORD. Why do women talk so much?

SALENA. They don't.

CLIFFORD. They don't? Okay. What age do you think she is?

SALENA. I have no idea. I never saw her face. Just eyes and nostrils. But she also had sunglasses on so I never really saw her eyes either.

CLIFFORD. Gosh, one neighbor covers her face with a pillowcase, and another one wears a pig's head. What kind of neighborhood have we moved into?

SALENA. I don't know. Oh you're looking worried again. Why don't you put your music back on?

CLIFFORD. Okay.

> *With his remote, he turns music on again. They both relax their bodies, feeling better.*

Scene 3

> *Back to the other house. Polly is watering the plant with a watering can. Timmy comes in from the kitchen.*

TIMMY. Be careful. He just got back.

POLLY. *(Baffled.)* What do you mean "be careful"?

> *Jimmy comes in. He is carrying what are presumably the guns in the black garbage bag. But he is not wearing the pig's head.*

(To Jimmy.) I finally found the potted plant. It was right here all along. Sometimes I can't see what's right in front of me. *(Noticing.)* Oh, what happened to the pig's head?

JIMMY. I threw it in the river.

POLLY. What river?

JIMMY. The river, the river!

POLLY. Well Timmy may want to use that Halloween pig's head again.

TIMMY. I don't. I never wore it, you bought it for me even though I told you I didn't want it but you didn't listen, you never listen, and I don't ever want to see the Pig's Head again.

POLLY. Well goodness sometimes he's so quiet, and then all of a sudden he's full of judgments. *(To Timmy.)* You're a child, wait until you're a grown-up before you judge others.

TIMMY. Did anything happen at the mall? There hasn't been anything on television.

JIMMY. You pipe down. This is a grown-up conversation.

POLLY. Well I meant to ask that too, but I was distracted by the plant. So tell us. Did you kill people?

JIMMY. Yes.

POLLY. No you didn't. You didn't kill yourself. You said you were going to do both.

JIMMY. I decided not to. I might write that novel. About a serial killer. And then if it gets published, maybe I'd win a Pulitzer Surprise. And if it doesn't get published, then I will kill myself, and you and Timmy too. But I am only on page one of the book, so you both have some time.

POLLY. Well that's good to know. I'm going to change my tune and encourage your procrastination from now on. Timmy, did you make any friends at school today?

TIMMY. No.

POLLY. How depressing you both are. I'm going to go upstairs and watch several episodes of *Project Runway*, to take my mind off things.

> *Polly exits up to the bedroom. Timmy goes to his room. Jimmy stands there. He looks at the plant. He goes up to it.*

JIMMY. *(To the plant.)* I hate you!

> *He takes one of the guns from his garbage bag. He aims the gun at the plant.*

(To the plant.) I hate all plants! I hate you! I hate you! *(Starts to pull the trigger.)* I hate you!

Quick blackout. We hear the sounds of the gun hitting the plant.

Scene 4

Clifford and Salena's house the next morning. Clifford is seated, looking a bit tense. He stands and starts to say affirmations aloud.

CLIFFORD. All is well. All is well. All is well. Everything is getting better. Everything is getting better. Everything is getting better.

(To audience.) I need to calm myself a lot. So I say "all is well" over and over. Although if it's a day where "all is well" seems like a great big whopping lie, then I shift to "Everything is getting better." Maybe also a lie. But it acknowledges that all is not well, but it suggests maybe things will get better.

I also have kind of stopped listening to the TV news.

(Giving a list of things usually on the news.) What horrible things have happened in the Middle East? How many beheadings and where? What 14-year-old has gone to school and shot twenty of his fellow students. How many airplanes are mysteriously missing in the ocean? Who's blowing up things in how many countries? How many tornados hit the Midwest for three days? Why is FedEx going to send us packages via drones flying through the air? When did that happen???

So lately I've stopped listening to the news entirely because I can feel my blood pressure going up. And my television has radio channels on it, including music stations with no talking. Of any kind. One channel is Frank Sinatra singing all the time. Actually he's like sixty percent of the time, but then there's Rosemary Clooney and Peggy Lee and Tony Bennett, and they're all very soothing, as well as dead. No Tony Bennett is still alive. And that channel helps me, but I've also started to listen much more to a classical music station.

And I didn't used to like classical music that much—but now I find that music written back then when people believed in God...

you know serfs and all, and the composers were inspired by the mammoth cathedrals, and they were always thinking about God when they were writing or sculpting or creating quartets...well the music was more orderly then, and more predictable, and your ear kind of knew what was coming next, and I didn't like it when I was younger but now that I feel the world is falling apart, well now I find that predictability of some of the music to be soothing.

Sometimes I look at the news for a minute, but then I switch to the classical music channel. And I can feel my blood pressure getting lower. And I start to feel calm.

> *Enter Salena.*

SALENA. You're talking to yourself again.

CLIFFORD. I guess so.

SALENA. Well Rosalind is coming by. So you'll get to meet her.

CLIFFORD. Oh I'm supposed to be at the paper.

SALENA. Well can't you be a little late? I really want you to meet her.

CLIFFORD. Oh well, there's not a specific meeting, I just feel I should show up there early from time to time. Especially as they're still getting used to me. But I guess I can be a little late.

SALENA. Oh good. She's coming over once she's done at the bus stop.

CLIFFORD. I wish I hadn't heard that gunfire around dinnertime yesterday.

SALENA. Well you said you saw the three of them walking around normally after the shots. So...maybe he was doing...target practice?

CLIFFORD. Well it sounded like inside the house—but even if he was outside doing "target practice," this is a suburban area, and the houses are close together. So there shouldn't be *anyone* doing target practice in their small back yard.

SALENA. Well I want to ask Rosalind what she knows about them, and maybe we should ask them over for a drink or something.

> *Enter Rosalind. She is dressed normally but she has a pillow-case over her head that goes down to her shoulders. There are holes in front of both of her eyes, and she has glasses over*

16

them. She has a small hole for her nostrils but not her nose. And she has a hole for her mouth too.

ROSALIND. Hello, the door was open, I hope you don't mind my just wandering in. I brought a coffee cake. It's from a mix. I don't know how to do anything from scratch.

SALENA. *(To Rosalind.)* Hi, Rosalind. This is Clifford.

CLIFFORD. Hello, nice to meet you.

ROSALIND. Thank you. Nice to meet you. Salena told me you work at the newspaper, that sounds like fun. Or maybe boring. Or maybe both.

CLIFFORD. It's actually both. Varies. Plus I've just started there.

ROSALIND. Do you mind if I take my pillowcase off?

SALENA. I'd love it.

ROSALIND. I'll just stay away from the windows.

She takes the pillowcase off her head; she looks normal but has two gauze bandages—one on her left cheek, and one on the left side of her neck.

These are new. I went to my dermatologist for a checkup, and he found two more basal cells, and so he took them off. Basal cells don't grow that fast, so that's good. Although it's disconcerting having little marks popping up on your face all the time. And the doctor uses the Mohs* surgery to get it off…do you know about that?

CLIFFORD. No I don't.

ROSALIND. Well they have to cut off the pimple-like thing on your face, but they try to take off the least amount of the skin underneath. And then you go to the waiting room and in forty-five minutes they put what was cut under a microscope and they can tell if they got all the cancer or not. And if they did, you get to go home. And if they didn't get it all, you go back to the chair, and they cut off some more of it, and then you wait. And each time if it isn't all gone, they cut a bit more. But that way they're sure they got everything.

The first time I had one, they got it after about two times. And sometimes it's only been once. Which is a happy day. But then one

_____
* Mohs is pronounced Moze.

of the times it went on for four cuttings… anyway, I just had no idea I was going to start getting these things every ten minutes.

CLIFFORD. I'm sorry to hear that.

ROSALIND. A lot of them are on the left side because if you drive, that's the side of your face that gets sun a lot. I mean I gave up sun-bathing when I was 30 or so…but I didn't realize that just walking around outside or driving the car, even in the winter, you can get these little cancer things. And I've gotten so many, I just don't want to keep getting any more. Ergo the pillowcase.

SALENA. Well that makes a lot of sense.

ROSALIND. I know it does. And I don't care if people look at me funny. I'm assuming the sun is stronger than it used to be since everything else in the world seems off. And I've been making poor Billy hold an umbrella over his head when we wait for the school bus because…well, the less sun rays you get the better, am I right?

CLIFFORD. You're right. Do the other children make fun of your son with the umbrella?

ROSALIND. No, Billy's very strong, nobody makes fun of him. They probably just say I'm crazy, but no, they don't make fun of Billy. Oh, that poor boy they keep calling Polly. I feel bad for him. He has that sensitivity that oozes out of his skin, and that always brings out the bully in the other children. Sensitivity is such a curse. I never had any. If someone is tailgating me and I'm going ten miles over the speed limit already and we're on winding roads, I look for a place to pull over, and let them go by, and then I tailgate them insanely, going really close, then pulling back, then really close again…until I disorient them enough so they drive off a cliff.

CLIFFORD. You haven't actually done that have you?

ROSALIND. No. I've thought of it. I haven't done it. I guess it's wrong to kill people.
(To both of them, but more to Clifford.) I feel I've been talking too much. *(To Clifford.)* Tell me something about you. What illnesses or physical problems do you have?

CLIFFORD. Oh, gosh. Just hard to get up in the morning.

ROSALIND. Is that a cry for help? I live with my father now and he was a psychologist, although he's retired, and he has arthritis and he's very angry about what's happening to the planet. He's furious about the arctic vortex. He thinks our only hope is if aliens from another planet come to Earth and they help us leave this planet, and take us to some other habitable planet where there's more space. So I don't know if he'd still be a good therapist. He's angry and forgets things and might be disturbing. But you could always just try one session.

CLIFFORD. Thank you, but I don't think so. I don't want therapy right now. And maybe I'll just wait for the aliens to come.

ROSALIND. Well it's an option.

CLIFFORD. Or it's a fantasy.

ROSALIND. Well that's what they say about chemtrails.

CLIFFORD. What?

SALENA. Should we eat some of the coffee cake?

ROSALIND. Sure, why not?

SALENA. I'll put it on some plates. I'll be right back.

Salena exits to the kitchen.

ROSALIND. She seems terrific. Knows just when to say "let's eat the coffee cake." I admire that. How long have you been married?

CLIFFORD. We're not married. We're just friends.

(Note: He doesn't want to give her information, whatever it is. He is private until he knows someone better. Also he is not thinking of sad things.)

ROSALIND. Oh. Were you ever married?

CLIFFORD. Yes. I'm not anymore.

ROSALIND. Children?

CLIFFORD. One.

ROSALIND. Girl or boy?

CLIFFORD. Boy.

ROSALIND. He's with his mother?

CLIFFORD. Yes, he's with his mother.

ROSALIND. How often do you see him?

CLIFFORD. You know, tell me about yourself. How long have you been wearing the pillowcase? Is your son one of the ones who picks on the child called Polly? Where's your husband?

ROSALIND. About six months. The pillowcase, I mean. And Billy *is* one of the ones who picks on the boy named Polly but I tell him not to, but his father was a bit of a bully himself, so I'm afraid it's a bit ingrained, part of genetics probably. And my husband—well fuck Facebook—his high school sweetheart tracked him down, she was unhappy with her life and her husband and she wanted to go back to an earlier time when she was prom queen or Cinderella at the ball or something, and my husband wanted to, you know, go back in time and follow the path not taken, and so the two of them are somewhere or other and I assume they're feeling young and vibrant because they've taken a time machine back to when they were 17 and they've wandered back in time reliving high school, I guess. And oh lucky, lucky them. And recently I've stopped hearing from him entirely.

CLIFFORD. Sorry. That sounds hard.

ROSALIND. Finding high school sweethearts happens on Facebook all the time. If you're 40 and up, it's the main point of having Facebook.

CLIFFORD. That's actually what happened to Salena. The exact same thing. Her husband hooked up with his high school sweetheart, and now they're together, and Salena is alone.

ROSALIND. Nothing works out, does it?

>*Enter Salena, carrying plates with coffee cake and coffee and tea.*

Salena! We're sisters! Facebook ruined our lives!

SALENA. What?

ROSALIND. Clifford told me your husband left you for his high school girlfriend. The same thing happened to me!

SALENA. Oh yes. Facebook. I didn't think of blaming Facebook. I thought more of blaming my husband.

ROSALIND. No, without Facebook you could have stayed in an unhappy marriage and not be alone.

SALENA. No… I'm kind of glad he left me. I mean at first I was upset, and felt insulted. But I wasn't really happy with him either. It was a wrong choice from the beginning.

20

ROSALIND. All three of us are not married! I think that's great! Good for us!

SALENA. Well…I guess good for us.

CLIFFORD. You know, I'm afraid I have to go to work.

ROSALIND. Why are you afraid?

CLIFFORD. I'm not. I'm just saying it's been nice to meet you, but I have to go to work.

SALENA. Wait. *(To Rosalind.)* Do you know the family next door to us?

ROSALIND. No, not really. I've seen them at a distance. And—oh—I think their son is the one everyone calls Polly.

SALENA. Cliff feels something's wrong with them, and I said we should ask them over for drinks. Would you be willing to be part of this? That way there are three of them, and three of us.

ROSALIND. Sure, I'd be glad to.

SALENA. Great.

CLIFFORD. I don't know. Maybe we shouldn't ask them over. Maybe we should leave them alone. Not stir the pot.

SALENA. No. You liked the idea earlier—maybe they're not as crazy as you think. Maybe the pig's head was about a joke at the office.

CLIFFORD. Okay fine. You choose a date. Good to meet you, Rosalind.

> *He exits, a bit abruptly.*

ROSALIND. Did I rub him the wrong way or something?

SALENA. No. He just takes a while to warm up.

ROSALIND. Yes I can see that. He really likes you though.

SALENA. Well we're good friends.

ROSALIND. Oh more than that.

SALENA. Oh I don't think so.

ROSALIND. Oh yes you do.

SALENA. Really, we're both getting over things, and it's comforting to be friends. Just friends.

ROSALIND. All right, I'll shut up. I'll change the topic. Why were you both talking about a pig's head.

SALENA. Oh Cliff was watching out the window, and the man next door was wearing a pig's head on his head, you know covering the whole head.

ROSALIND. Oh. Well, maybe he's protecting himself from rays of the sun. Or he has a sense of humor. Or he's crazy.

SALENA. Yes. One of those.

They both worry a little bit...

Scene 5

The house of Polly and Jimmy and Timmy. Polly is seated, drinking coffee. She addresses the audience.

POLLY. So he killed the plant. That makes me so mad. What has the plant ever done to him? And I liked giving it water and sustenance and helping it live. And now he's gone and killed it. I mean that's going a little too far for me.

I mean I used to think it was fine not to have background checks to get a gun. I mean what if you need a gun really fast and all, and somebody breaks into your house and just because sometime someone sent you to a mental hospital for a while or gave you shock treatments or something, that's no reason not to be able to get a gun in case somebody breaks into your house. I mean you have a right to protect yourself.

But killing a plant that I loved...well I think maybe he shouldn't be allowed to have a gun, if he's not going to use it sensibly.

Maybe I *should* call the police, and tell them he shot my plant. But then I don't want the whole neighborhood to think we're crazy. And of course God will protect us from harm. Although he didn't protect the plant. But maybe God doesn't value plants as much as I do.

Oh the Olympics. A path not taken. I'm a good person, aren't I? I think I am. And I want to go to heaven. I want to die in my sleep, maybe earlier than expected—say, 65—maybe I'd like to go to heaven around that time. And I'd like to just die quietly in my sleep, no big deal, no doctors, just suddenly I'm dead.

And oh won't that be wonderful. I bet when you get there… I don't know if it's St. Peter at the Gates—*maybe* it's St. Peter and *maybe* he's at the Gates—but I'm hoping he doesn't have some sort of typical harp or something. I'm hoping he's in charge of some big fancy Red Carpet up in heaven, just like the Golden Globes and the Oscars, and a whole bunch of us are in evening gowns…and the men are in tuxedos, and we're being welcomed and applauded!

And Joan Rivers is dead now, poor thing, but she's up in heaven now, saying who's the best dressed, and who's the worst dressed. And who are you wearing? She created that question. That's such a funny phrase. Who are you wearing? I'm wearing Oscar de la Renta, Joan, I'd say.

And then Joan would say, are you wearing a dress *designed* by him, or are you actually *wearing* him? And then because heaven is a magical place, I would say to her, I am actually *wearing* him. The dress is him wrapped around me, and it both looks like a dress, and it also looks like a person, a famous person.

And in heaven some people on the Red Carpet are traditional and just wearing the designer dresses like you would at the Oscars. But some people like me, who are more imaginative, well we are wearing the actual designers. And because it's heaven, maybe the Red Carpet goes on for…several years. Or there's no time limit at all.

And then suddenly my dress changes, and I say to Joan, I am no longer wearing Oscar de la Renta, I'm now wearing Dolce and Gabbana. And in the front of me I'm wearing Mr. Dolce and in the back of me I'm wearing Mr. Gabbana. And I feel very special.

    Enter Jimmy, grouchy.

JIMMY. What garbage are you talking now?

POLLY. I am thinking of spiritual matters, and what happens up in heaven. Where I will go. And which, unless you change your behavior, you will not be going there. You will go to hell, and burn for eternity. I don't say that with anger, I just think that's probably where you'll end up.

JIMMY. The book isn't going very well. I don't think I know how to write. I'm getting depressed.

POLLY. I have happy fantasies of going to heaven, and wearing Oscar de la Renta. Why can't you have happy fantasies like that?

JIMMY. I used to fantasize about Julia Roberts, and she was in love with me and everyone in the world was envious of me with such a beautiful wife. But then you made me watch that awful chick flick with her in it, and you ruined Julia Roberts for me. That's why I can't have happy fantasies anymore. What was that movie called?

POLLY. *Eat, Pray, Love.* And it was a very spiritual book, and I wanted to see the movie, but when we rented it you got so angry you tried to push me out the window.

JIMMY. It was a terrible movie. No normal man in his right mind would ever like that movie. Or the book. Eat, pray, love. Praying is a waste of time, love doesn't exist. And eating triggers your body functions and then you shit in the toilet.

POLLY. You are disgusting. Do you know that? D-I-S-G-U-S-T-I-N-G. Thank God Timmy doesn't take after you.

JIMMY. Well of course he doesn't.

POLLY. Well it's a lucky thing.

JIMMY. He was adopted, so how could he be like me.

POLLY. Well you're the male example, and we don't know who his real parents were. But if the mother was nice and the father was terrible like you, then Timmy might grow up to be a criminal and a psychopath.

> *She speaks to the audience.*

Don't tell Timmy. He doesn't know he's adopted. I wouldn't want him to think he wasn't wanted by his real parents.

JIMMY. Who are you talking to?

POLLY. I'm talking to Joan Rivers, and I'm wearing Oscar de la Renta.

JIMMY. What?

POLLY. You don't understand anything I say, do you? And I'm glad I couldn't conceive with you. It would be terrifying to have your genes floating around the country.

JIMMY. Oh yeah? Well I want you to know that before I married you, I gave buckets and buckets of my jism to a sperm bank. They paid me for it. How do you like that?

POLLY. Oh Lord. I was having such a nice fantasy of when I'm in heaven, and then you come in here and change the atoms in the room, and I don't know. I think you're beyond St. John's wort. AND YOU HAVEN'T APOLOGIZED FOR KILLING MY PLANT!

JIMMY. Apologize. You have ruined my life, and everyone in the world has ruined my life and so I don't apologize to anyone.

POLLY. I loved that plant!

Phone rings.

Hello? Yes. Uh-huh. Yes. Oh. That would be nice. Tomorrow? What time? That would be lovely. Thank you.
(To Jimmy.) We've been invited to a cocktail party next door.

Jimmy stares at her, blank and somewhat confused. Then he starts to choke her. Not enough to kill her, but just he's annoyed. He doesn't want to meet any neighbors.

Timmy comes in.

TIMMY. What are you doing? Stop it!!!!

Jimmy stops after a few moments. Polly holds her throat.

JIMMY. Your mother was saying hateful things to me.

TIMMY. You both should be put into a mental hospital.

POLLY. Oh Timmy, don't take it so hard. He wasn't really choking me. He was just expressing himself, and he's not good with words. Your mother and father are very difficult, but we mean well. And your father hasn't had his coffee yet this morning. Jimmy, why don't you go back and see if you can write any more. Today's the day I'm starting home schooling with Timmy.

JIMMY. Eat, pray, love, vomit.

POLLY. You are so hostile.

JIMMY. I think that could be my first sentence. Let me go write that down.

He exits.

POLLY. Oh well that's encouraging. Remember as long as he keeps writing the book he isn't going to kill people at the mall. Now I was going to cover subtraction and addition this morning, but I have a headache and my neck hurts. So why don't you watch *The View* and

25

write a report on it. And then I'll read it later, and that can be our learning session today. All right?

He stares at her.

I asked you to do a report on *The View*. Can you say yes or no please?

TIMMY. All right. I will give you an oral report on *The View*.

POLLY. All right. See how flexible I am.

TIMMY. *(Sympathetic.)* I'm sorry about your plant, Mom.

POLLY. *(Moved.)* Oh. Thank you.

She hugs him, exits. He looks after her, and then stares ahead.

Scene 6

Clifford and Salena's house. Clifford is pacing a bit.

SALENA. Do you have to pace? It's making me nervous.

CLIFFORD. Oh I'm just anxious about us having invited them.

SALENA. Well you didn't hear gunshots yesterday, that was a good thing.

CLIFFORD. Yes, I guess so.

Doorbell.

Oh they're here.

Both Clifford and Salena open the door.

Hello.

SALENA. Welcome.

POLLY. Hi, I'm Polly. Thanks for inviting us.

Clifford and Salena lead Polly into the room. Jimmy and Timmy are a bit behind Polly.

SALENA. Well it's good to meet you.

POLLY. And these are my two men, Jimmy and Timmy.

SALENA. And I'm Salena, and this is Clifford.

POLLY. Hello. Can you guess who Timmy is and who Jimmy is?

SALENA. Not really.

JIMMY. I'm Jimmy. And it's not a game, Polly. *(Looks irritatedly at Polly.)*

POLLY. "Polly Polly Oxen Free!" That's what they said when I was little and playing hide and seek. I didn't understand it was "Ollie Ollie," I thought it was "Polly Polly." Those were happy times.

CLIFFORD. Oh, well—hello, Jimmy. *(To Timmy.)* And you must be Timmy.

JIMMY. *(Said as if Clifford is an idiot.)* Duh!

> Everyone is quiet for a moment.

SALENA. Uh, would anyone like a drink?

JIMMY. I would like a glass of whiskey.

POLLY. Jimmy is an alcoholic but I think he can drink today because he's shy with company.

JIMMY. I'm not an alcoholic!

POLLY. Yes you are.

JIMMY. I'm not.

POLLY. Well that policeman said you were.

JIMMY. No he said I was drunk, not an alcoholic. And I drank too much because you wouldn't stop talking.

POLLY. Well I remember him calling you an alcoholic. We'll discuss it later.

JIMMY. Much later. After you're dead.

SALENA. I'm not sure what to do. Do I get him whiskey?

POLLY. Yes, he can fall off the wagon occasionally.

JIMMY. That's right, I can. *(To Clifford.)* You're very quiet.

CLIFFORD. Sorry, I guess am. *(Trying to be nice to him, he hopes.)* Um, I'm shy with new people too.

JIMMY. What do you mean "too"?

CLIFFORD. Well your wife said you're shy with new people, and I'm kind of that way too. Like you.

JIMMY. You're nothing like me. Why do you have a black wife?

CLIFFORD. Uh…uh…

SALENA. Oh my. I feel light-headed. Let me sit down.

She sits and puts her head between her knees.

POLLY. Jimmy, look what you've done to this poor woman.

JIMMY. I didn't do anything to her.

POLLY. *(To Clifford and Salena.)* I think we have gotten off on the wrong foot. And we should go outside and then come back in, and start all over again. Okay?

> *She doesn't wait for a response, but kind of pushes Jimmy and Timmy out the door they came in through. Salena and Clifford both look at the closed door they just left through. There's a bit of a pause.*

CLIFFORD. Are they coming back?

SALENA. Well that's what she said. *(Whispering a bit.)* I kind of hope maybe they won't come back, but I feel they probably will.

> *They wait some more. Wondering what the delay is.*
>
> *Suddenly there is a shriek outside. Then we hear Rosalind speaking to them.*

ROSALIND. *(Offstage.)* I'm sorry, I didn't mean to scare you. Did I scare you? I'm Roz. It's about the sun. I didn't mean to scare you. Did you just get here?

POLLY. *(Offstage.)* No we were in already, but we're starting over.

ROSALIND. What do you mean, starting over?

> *The people outside start to come in now—Polly, Rosalind, Jimmy, and Timmy. They come into the house.*

POLLY. *(Addresses Clifford and Salena.)* Hello, you must be Clifford and Sobia.

SALENA. Salena…

POLLY. Oh sorry. Why couldn't you call yourself Mary? Don't answer that, it's a joke. I think Salena is a lovely name. And Sobia too. *(Points to Jimmy and Timmy.)* And this is my husband Jimmy, and this is my son Polly.

JIMMY. His name isn't Polly.

POLLY. *(To Timmy.)* Oh sorry, darling. I just get confused. *(To Clifford and Salena.)* My son's name is… oh Lord, I'm going blank.

JIMMY. His name rhymes with Jimmy.

28

POLLY. Oh yes of course. It rhymes with Jimmy. Gosh I still don't have it. Gimme, gimme. Kimmy kimmy. Shimmy shimmy cocoa puff

TIMMY. MY NAME IS TIMMY! TIMMY, TIMMY!

POLLY. Oh yes, of course. I'm so sorry. And Gimme and Shimmy aren't really names, are they? I wonder if *I* should go outside and come in again.

SALENA. No. Don't do that. Let's just move forward from here.

POLLY. All right. That sounds like a very nice idea. And what's his name again? I'm forgetting it again.

CLIFFORD. His name is Timmy.

POLLY. Oh yes, thank you. It's all this anxiety about when you get to go to heaven. And of course the death of my plant.

CLIFFORD. Ah. I see.

He doesn't.

SALENA. And Rosalind, don't you want to take off your…hat?

ROSALIND. What hat? It's a pillowcase.

She takes it off.

JIMMY. Pillowcase, huh. Does that mean you're a member of the Ku Klux Klan? *(To Salena.)* You wouldn't like that, would you?

SALENA. You're correct. I wouldn't like someone from the Ku Klux Klan in my house.

JIMMY. They burn crosses on Halloween, right?

SALENA. Uh…no not really.

ROSALIND. No, no, I'm not a Ku Klux Klan person. I wear this pillowcase to block the sun because of my multiple basal cells on my face. Do you know what Mohs surgery is?

POLLY. No, what is it? It sounds like fun.

ROSALIND. *(Pause.)* Well it's not "fun" but come over here, and let me tell you about it privately because the audience has already heard about it.

Rosalind goes upstage and Polly, Jimmy, and Timmy follow her. She explains it to them softly, we don't hear her or them.

Clifford and Salena stay downstage and talk, quietly so the

29

others don't hear them speaking.

CLIFFORD. I told you we shouldn't have asked them over.

SALENA. Well they're here now.

CLIFFORD. That poor kid is living in a loony bin. Neither one of his parents make any sense. And the guy is frightening.

SALENA. Maybe the husband is like an excitable dog, and as he calms down and gets some treats, maybe he'll become more normal.

> *Jimmy hears this from upstage and looks down, annoyed. He's heard Salena, mostly has not heard Clifford. And Rosalind, Polly, and Timmy haven't heard either one.*

JIMMY. I am not a dog!

SALENA. I didn't say you were.

JIMMY. Yes you did.

SALENA. No you misunderstood. It was a metaphor. It was a compliment, I said with time maybe you'd feel more…comfortable with us.

JIMMY. How am I like a dog? Did I bite your hand? Did I pee on your leg?

POLLY. What's being said? I'm confused. I was so fascinated by the Moses surgery, that I was thinking of the parting of the Red Sea and how lovely it is to see *The Ten Commandments* on TV at Easter. And to me Charlton Heston IS Moses. And Easter is just as important as Christmas, but it doesn't get as much attention, does it? I never understood what those little yellow marshmallow chicks had to do with anything. I mean it's about the holy time of Easter with Jesus on the Cross and then He dies, and then Sunday He's alive again. Which is what Easter is about, right? It's not a metaphor for marshmallows, is it?

SALENA. What? Uh, no, I guess it's not.

JIMMY. This black lady has been saying I'm like a dog.

POLLY. Stop referring to the color of her skin, would you, Jimmy? I don't understand how you became this way. Who were your parents, did I ever meet them?

JIMMY. Yeah you met them. My father was like a dog, and my mother was a bitch.

POLLY. Jimmy STOP IT. All right, thanks to you, we have to go outside AGAIN and come back in. Come on, you two. And Timmy, you could talk more, and Jimmy you could talk less.

> *Polly drags Jimmy and Timmy outside again. There is a long pause in the room among Clifford, Salena, and Rosalind.*

CLIFFORD. How are we going to get out of this?

> *Slight pause before anyone can speak. Then Polly, Jimmy and Timmy come back in.*

POLLY. Hello. How nice to meet all of you, for the first time. It's so nice of you to…to…to… Oh God my brain is going blank for a moment. So nice of you to invite us to dinner. I mean cocktails. Or even just a glass of water. We don't need much. It's lovely to meet you. I'm Polly, and this is my husband Jimmy, and just to make it easy to remember, my son's name is Timmy, although we like to call him Polly. I'm sorry we don't call him Polly, it's the mean children at school who call him Polly, not me and his father. And his father had a terrible time in school too, but let's not bring that up. And plus he was a juvenile and so his record was expunged. So it's all gone. *(Sort of happy.)* All gone! *(To Rosalind.)* You know, why don't you finish what you were saying about the Moses surgery. I would like to hear more about it.

ROSALIND. All right. It's not Moses. It's Mohs surgery. M-O-H-S.

POLLY. No that's not how you spell Moses. It's spelled M-O-S-E-S. Moses.

ROSALIND. Yes but I'm not spelling Moses.

POLLY. I know you're not. You're spelling it wrong. I remember from the TV Guide how to spell the name "Moses." That movie is on every Easter.

ROSALIND. Okay. That's fine. I think I don't want to explain any more about the MOHS surgery. *(Enunciates MOHS, still trying to explain.)*

> *Polly is looking annoyed and feeling misunderstood. Salena decides to intervene.*

SALENA. Let's not talk about cancer anymore and let's just be glad it's not one of the scarier cancers…

ROSALIND. Well if I keep getting them over and over, eventually I won't have a face.

31

SALENA. Well I think you're doing well protecting yourself with the pillowcase. But we haven't brought out any beverages, it's very rude of us. But if you don't mind, I'm going to make an executive decision, and not serve any alcohol today, let's just have sodas and sparkling water and tea with lemon. Does that sound good?

JIMMY. So you don't have any whiskey?

SALENA. No we don't. I forgot that we don't have it. Sorry.

JIMMY. *(To Polly.)* God, how long do I have to stay here?

SALENA. *(With an edge.)* You know what, why don't I get you a soda, and you can scarf it down as fast as ever you can, and then you can *leave*. Does that sound good??? I'll go get the sodas.

POLLY. I'd like the sparkling water, if you don't mind.

SALENA. *(A bit nicer to Polly.)* Yes, absolutely. Delightful.

> Salena exits to kitchen. Everyone is silent for a bit. Looking around at each other. Unable to think what to say. After a while Rosalind speaks.

ROSALIND. It must be twenty minutes after the hour. Angels are here.

> Polly, Jimmy, and Timmy all look confused.

CLIFFORD. *(Decides to explain it.)* It's a superstition. That's when people are together, and they suddenly fall silent, it's because they suddenly sense angels in the room, and it always seems to happen on twenty minutes after the hour.

TIMMY. I don't think we have angels in our house. I wish we did.

CLIFFORD. Well maybe they're there, and you're just not able to sense them.

POLLY. I often think of heaven. I find it comforting, and I do believe I'm going to heaven. I was imagining talking to Joan Rivers on the red carpet in heaven. I don't know that there is one, although maybe Joan Rivers might make it happen up there.

CLIFFORD. That's a very imaginative thought you had.

POLLY. Thank you. What do you do for a living?

CLIFFORD. Uh, we moved here because I got a job as an assistant editor at the local paper. In the past, I was actually the editor of a newspaper, but I took a couple of years off, and I thought I should...

go slower, not work as hard.

JIMMY. I'm writing a book.

CLIFFORD. Oh? You are?

JIMMY. Yes I am. I think it's a good idea. Polly and Joan Rivers aren't the only ones with an imagination. I have imagination.

POLLY. Well time will tell. He used to be a truck driver. But he stopped that a few months ago.

JIMMY. I kept falling asleep at the wheel.

CLIFFORD. *(Starting to be upset.)* Did you hit anyone?

JIMMY. I don't know. I guess if I did I would've woken up. I had a lot of blackouts. So they won't let me drive a truck anymore.

CLIFFORD. *(He's having trouble talking.)* …my…my…wife and son…were killed. By a truck driver. Who fell asleep.

> *Clifford didn't mean to talk…or didn't intend to say this. He wants to get out of the room, and he leaves through the main door, going to his car. They all stare after him. Silent.*
>
> *Salena comes back with assorted sodas and a glass of sparkling water.*

SALENA. Sorry I've been so long. *(Notices.)* Where is Cliff?

> *No one knows how to explain. Maybe some energetic classical music comes on? Lights dim.*

Scene 7

> *Polly and Timmy are in their main room. It's the next day. (Is it morning, and Polly is in a bathrobe? To make it clear it's early morning?)*

POLLY. There goes the schoolbus. In a little while we should start the homeschooling again, we missed yesterday. It was such an upsetting day. I wonder if your father is going to sleep all day. I think he was very upset by it.

TIMMY. I want to go back to school.

POLLY. Yes but they all call you Polly.

TIMMY. Not all of them. The teachers don't call me Polly. Some of the girls don't. Well they don't talk to me at all, they sort of whisper to one another. But there's this one girl, Jessica, and she says hello to me. She says, "Hello, Timmy." And if any of the boys are nearby, she says "Hello, Timmy" really loud, and looks at the boys as if to say "What's the matter with you?" And then they all say in unison, "Timmy has a girlfriend but it's only because she feels sorry for him." And then there's one girl whose name is Polly for real, and she really doesn't like it that they call me Polly, because she keeps thinking they're talking to her, and then she realizes no one is talking to her. Once I said to her, "It's hard for the both of us being called Polly. We should be called Polly 1 and Polly 2." I thought that was funny. But she just said "Oh shut up," and we've never spoken since.

POLLY. Well I think they're all terrible, and we treat you much better here.

> *Enter Jimmy. He is wearing a dress somewhat similar to what Rosalind wore yesterday. And he has a pillowcase on his head, just like Rosalind's—with opening for his mouth and eyes. And he's also wearing sunglasses, as Rosalind did originally.*

JIMMY. How do I look?

POLLY. *(Truly upset.)* Oh God. Is this one of those Caitlyn Jenner makeover things or something?

JIMMY. What? Who?

POLLY. I mean our marriage has so much wrong with it, and you go over to the neighbors and you prove yourself to be mentally unable to talk to anybody, and then you make the host break down and have to leave the house…and if NOW you're going to go ahead and change your whole gender, well then, I don't know what to do. When is all this craziness going to stop, Jimmy?

JIMMY. What are you talking about? I'm dressed this way because I'm going to the mall to kill people and probably kill myself, but if I only kill a few people, I might decide not to kill myself, and thus I want my face to be covered.

POLLY. Why don't you stick with the pig's head?

JIMMY. Why can't you retain anything? I threw the pig's head in the river.

POLLY. What river?

JIMMY. The river, the river!

POLLY. *(To Timmy.)* I'm not aware of any river nearby, are you, Timmy?

TIMMY. No I'm not.

JIMMY. Did I say it was nearby? Did I?

POLLY. Well I assumed it. Why would you choose to drive miles to throw out a pig's head?

JIMMY. I just felt like driving. I wanted to get rid of it so no one would connect it to me. Plus I miss driving my truck, and I've been having trouble sleeping, so I wondered if I drove for a while, maybe I'd fall asleep on the road, and I could finally get some shut-eye.

> *(Note: Jimmy may lift up his pillowcase from time to time but much of the time he leaves it on. Unless that's not good for the scene…)*

POLLY. Fall asleep at the wheel? What is going on with you? I've tried to be optimistic that you mean well, on some level, and that you'll get better. But it's all adding up in a bad way. Just like when you insisted I drive with you, and then you drove us off a great bridge and we sunk into this river and…oh was it that river?

JIMMY. Yes that river.

POLLY. Oh it's a very pretty bridge. If I were a photographer, I'd take photos of it. Maybe I should give up my hopes for the Olympics, and I should become a photographer.

JIMMY. Yeah, you and who else? Why don't you go to the mall and I'll shoot you there, and then you'll see what happens when the world comes to an end.

POLLY. Jimmy, you're not making sense today. Something happened to you yesterday at that awful so-called cocktail party. You went crazy. Or crazier. Darling, I want you to go back to writing your novel. Remember you said as long as you were writing the novel, you wouldn't go out and kill anyone. Do you remember that agreement?

JIMMY. *(Lifts his pillowcase up for a bit.)* I don't know how to write. I only have three sentences.

POLLY. Well…build on that, darling. What are the sentences?

JIMMY. "Eat Pray Love Vomit." "Kill people at the mall." "Trees are beautiful."

POLLY. Well the last one is very nice. Why don't you make that be the first sentence? And build on that?

JIMMY. But none of the words connect. I don't know how to write.

He puts the pillowcase back on his face.

POLLY. Well I think you just need to move them around a bit. And think happier thoughts. We don't want to hear the word "vomit" in the first sentence. Or any sentence. Why don't you start with "Trees are beautiful." Then you can say, "I like to eat. I like to pray. I like to love." And then the "Kill people at the mall" sentence, I would cut out entirely. Or you could make it more friendly, and say "I like to make friends at the mall."

JIMMY. Those are all your thoughts, they're not mine. If I copied what you said, well it wouldn't be true to how I feel. And I hate what you wrote. It's goody-goody.

POLLY. I'm a woman, so I have a lot of empathy. Maybe you need a man to help you with your writing. That neighbor next door is a writer, he works at a newspaper, he used to be an editor.

JIMMY. Are you kidding? He thinks I killed his wife and son. Why would he possibly help me?

POLLY. Darling, he didn't think you had killed his family. The fact you drove a truck and sometimes fell asleep while driving, well that just REMINDED him of what happened, and that made him sad. Did you miss that communication, dear?

JIMMY. What? No he said I killed them, and I didn't.

POLLY. I don't think that's correct. I felt sad for the man. Imagine losing your child and your spouse. Can you feel empathy for him, Jimmy?

TIMMY. *(To his father, suddenly and loudly.)* WHY DO YOU HAVE THAT Pillowcase ON YOUR HEAD?

POLLY. Good God, that was so loud. Timmy, you go for hours and don't say anything and then all of a sudden you scream your head off. What were you learning in that public school we sent you to? Thank goodness we've switched you to homeschooling. Which reminds me, Jimmy, we need to stop this conversation. Today I need to teach Timmy about the Puritans landing on Plymouth Rock.

TIMMY. You don't have any validation to be teaching homeschooling.

POLLY. Well that's not what the principal said.

TIMMY. What did she say?

POLLY. She mentioned validation but then she said just go away and leave me alone, I never want to see you ever again. Most people like me. I don't know what's the matter with your principal.

JIMMY. Oh I forgot something.

He exits into another room.

POLLY. All right. Now where was I?

She is paraphrasing something.

Okay. School time.

It seems that times have changed in various ways. And sometimes we put the clock backwards, and sometimes we put the clock forward. And sometimes we had to rewind the clock, and apparently that gave the Puritans quite a shock when it was 1620 and they were in a boat that landed on Plymouth Rock. Many years later, in the 1920s, if the Puritans had a terrible cold and coughed up phlegm, instead of landing on Plymouth Rock, Plymouth Rock would land on them.

TIMMY. What are you talking about?

POLLY. I'm talking about the Puritans and when they colonized America, and they created turkey and Thanksgiving. What part were you not understanding?

Jimmy comes back in, still with the pillowcase on his head. But now he's carrying his assault rifles, and is also carrying big garbage bags he will put the rifles into.

Oh, darling, you have your automatic rifles again.

JIMMY. I give up on the book, you ruined it for me by changing all the words and making them your words. And I can't figure what to do with my life, so I'm going to the mall and I'll either be back if my mood lightens or else I'll be dead and so will other random people.

POLLY. Please just go back to bed, would you?

TIMMY. I'm sorry. We have to call the police.

JIMMY. *(Very threatening.)* What did you just say?

Everyone freezes. Lights dim quickly.

Scene 8

The same morning, but at Clifford and Salena's house. Clifford is alone, sitting with coffee. He's kind of shut down from yesterday. He picks up a remote near him, and aims it at the TV in front of him.* He and we hear the morning news.

CLIFFORD. *(Turns off the TV entirely.)* All is well. No, that's definitely not true. Um, things are getting better all the time. That's also not true. Um. I am all right at this moment. I am all right at this moment. Yes, that's true. I am all right.

Salena comes in.

Oh God the news is like hell.

SALENA. I told you to stop watching.

CLIFFORD. So much of the violence is so unpredictable. A stranger goes to a movie house and kills people. Someone angry that you honked at them, then they kill you. Or just someone falls asleep at the wheel and then they hit Rebecca and Andrew.

SALENA. You haven't said their names in a long while.

CLIFFORD. I try not to, I guess. Did you ever see the movie *The Razor's Edge*? Tyrone Power is looking for the meaning of life—I think he found it but I'm not sure what it was—but meanwhile Anne Baxter had a supporting role—she even won an Oscar—and she was this woman who got married and had a child, and they were all in a car crash, and only she survived. The husband and child were dead. They have a scene where they tell her. And then she

---

* The TV is not really seen. Clifford aims the remote toward the audience, as if that is the TV.

disappears from the film and later she's in Paris and she's become an opium addict. Anything to blot everything out I guess.

SALENA. Gosh you watch so many old movies.

CLIFFORD. Do you think they have opium dens in America? Where would I find one?

SALENA. Did you do your "all is well" affirmations today?

CLIFFORD. I tried. I just couldn't believe it.

SALENA. I'm going to make you a calming cup of tea.

> *She exits.*

CLIFFORD. No I want an opium den.

> *He looks out the window.*

Oh. There's Rosalind. Except she's coming out of the crazy people's house. And she's going to the man's car. Oh Lord. It's not Rosalind, it's the crazy man wearing a dress and a pillowcase on his head. Salena, come look! Oh, and now he's driving away.

> *Enter Salena.*

SALENA. What are you shouting about?

CLIFFORD. I think that crazy man has dressed himself like Rosalind, and I don't know what's up with him.

SALENA. He's just crazy. Can't we just ignore him? Or I wonder if we should just move?

CLIFFORD. I was thinking the same thing. Except we just got the house a month ago, it seems crazy to leave so soon. And if we move somewhere else, there might be someone even crazier next door. Or maybe we'd move and the neighbors would be fine, but then some small private plane will fly toward the house and lose control, and they'll crash the plane and wreck the house, and we'll either die because the house blows up, or if we don't die, in any case we'll be homeless. Or maybe some people will start attacking the house with drones. Why can people buy drones, do you know? It sort of just happened one day. Everything is so unpredictable. The house will be gone and we'll drive to some motel, but then on the way there, someone will fall asleep driving their truck, and they'll crash into us, and we'll be dead. There are too many horrible things that can happen. So many options for disaster.

SALENA. Cliff. Dear. Your brain is spinning into…mental chaos. You're fine now. Everything is fine now. Isn't that right?

CLIFFORD. Sure. Why not? Everything is fine now. I just don't want to have a scary neighbor.

Salena looks out the window.

SALENA. Oh Cliff. Good news. It actually is Rosalind. Somehow you thought it was Crazy Jimmy, but it was Roz.

Doorbell. Offstage:

ROSALIND. Can I come in?

SALENA. Yes please do. Cliff thought he saw the crazy neighbor dressed up like you, so would you please tell him you're you and not him.

ROSALIND. Yes I'm me. I'm not the crazy neighbor.

SALENA. See, Cliff. Really, honey, you have to stop your brain from jumping to terrible fears of what might go wrong. I mean, I know sometimes bad things happen, but you shouldn't jump to all your worst fears.

ROSALIND. I'm afraid he's right about the neighbor. I was looking out my window, and darn if I didn't see someone dressed up just like me with a pillowcase on his head.
And he got in his car and he drove away.

SALENA. Oh. *(To Clifford.)* Sorry. I gave this long song and dance not to imagine things, but you were right.

CLIFFORD. That's all right. I wish you were right, and I was wrong. But now there are two pillowcased people in the neighborhood.

ROSALIND. Why is he dressed up like me? Is he going to rob a bank, and somehow blame it on me?

CLIFFORD. You know what. Let's go next door and ask that woman— what's her name again?

SALENA. Polly.

CLIFFORD. Let's all of us go next door. If he's going to pass himself off as Roz, we have a right to ask what he's doing.

SALENA. Oh God. I can just imagine what gobbledygook she'll blather at us…

CLIFFORD. Come on, let's go over…

The three of them head to the door...

Scene 9

The house next door. Polly and Timmy are seated back-to-back in chairs, and they are tied up by rope so they can't move. They are tied up around the torso and around the feet, and their mouths are covered with tape.

Polly is talking endlessly, although the tape around her mouth makes her impossible to understand. But she's talking away. Timmy rolls his eyes from time to time, wondering what the hell his mother could be saying at this point, tied up and with her mouth taped shut.

POLLY. *(We can't understand any words, but her eyes and intonation are active; she's saying real thoughts.)* Bllllllgggg huuuuuu waaaaaaaaah wahhhhhhhh plaaahhhhh quaaaaaa twng bllllllggg stannnnnggggg bobbbbbbb... *(Etc.)*

    Doorbell. Polly makes more noises. After a bit, Clifford, Salena, and Rosalind come into the house, the door is unlocked. The three of them are shocked to see Polly and Timmy tied up.

SALENA. Oh my God!

    Clifford and Salena go about untying them, and taking the tape off their mouths. Rosalind flutters from one to other, not quite sure how to help.

ROSALIND. Oh Lord Lord. Why is he dressed like me? Is he going to rob a bank?

CLIFFORD. Are you both okay?

POLLY. Well I couldn't talk! He put tape on my mouth. I tried to talk but you can't form words that way.

CLIFFORD. Uh-huh. Where is Jimmy?

POLLY. Well he's right here.

TIMMY. *(Really fed up with mother.)* No! I'm Timmy, not Jimmy. God, put the tape back on her mouth.

CLIFFORD. Where is your father?

TIMMY. Father left with guns and was wearing a pillowcase just like Rosalind.

POLLY. Timmy, you're 13, you shouldn't call a grown-up by their first name, you should be polite and call her Mrs. …Something or other. What is your last name, Roz, I guess I don't know it.

ROSALIND. O'Shawnessy. I've gone back to my maiden name.

CLIFFORD. *(To Polly.)* Where did your husband go?

POLLY. Oh who knows. I can't keep up with him. He tied us up, you know.

TIMMY. And she helped him to tie me up. They did it together.

CLIFFORD. What? Why?

POLLY. Well I was protecting Timmy. Timmy, I was protecting you. Your father got so ANGRY when you said we should call the police about him. I mean he looked furious. So when he wanted me to tie you up, I thought I was protecting you because when Jimmy saw that you couldn't call the police, I thought he'd stop feeling threatened and then I could offer him whiskey and a couple of Valiums, and then he'd probably fall asleep. And then everything would have been fine. I had no idea he would tie me up too.

CLIFFORD. Stop talking, would you?

POLLY. Well it's my house, you know.

CLIFFORD. Timmy's right, we have to call the police right away.

POLLY. Well I suppose so. Although I have no idea where he went.

TIMMY. Well he usually talked about killing people at the mall, right?

POLLY. There are a lot of malls, Timmy.

TIMMY. Well the closest one is the Calvin Felletti Mall.

POLLY. Oh I love Calvin Klein. I could wear him on the red carpet.

TIMMY. It's Calvin Felletti.

POLLY. Who is Calvin Felletti?

TIMMY. He's the rich man who built the mall. But then he killed himself.

POLLY. Oh I long to go to heaven.

ROSALIND. I'm feeling very nervous for some reason. Do you mind if I dance?

Rosalind starts to do an Isadora Duncan–like dance in the background; she does it fairly well and has a long scarf she can move around. Everyone stares at her. Clifford and Salena exchange glances, but decide to ignore it; her dancing is unusual but benign.

POLLY. Well we don't know if he's at the Fettuccini Mall or not. There are other malls nearby. Plus he's always driving miles and miles to that bridge in some county where he throws things in a river. You know it's the same bridge he drove into the river trying to drown us, but both times our windows were open and so we were able to swim out. He doesn't think ahead.

CLIFFORD. I'm sorry, we're wasting time, we have to call the police.

SALENA. I just had a horrible thought. He may have started killing people already. Let's turn on the TV and see if there's anything about it.

Polly aims the remote, and everyone looks ahead as if the TV is in front of them.

The Lifetime channel doesn't have local news. We need channel 33.

POLLY. Oh I never watch 33.

SALENA. Well today's a day to start.

Channel is switched.

VOICE FROM TV. So far there have been seven people killed, and twenty people wounded...

Everyone is greatly shocked. Still looking at the TV. Rosalind stops her dancing, pays attention...

CLIFFORD. Oh my God. He's already started it.

TIMMY. I recognize it. It's the Calvin Felletti mall.

SALENA. Oh God.

POLLY. *(To Clifford.)* You should have called the police from your house instead of coming over here to do God knows what.

CLIFFORD. Well we untied you. And I didn't know what he was doing. If he was threatening to kill people, *you* should have called the police weeks ago.

SALENA. You have a child in the house. And you did nothing about his threats? You could have been killed.

POLLY. Why would I be killed?

TIMMY. You are an idiot.

POLLY. That's a cruel thing to say to your mother. You should wait until you're 18 to say something like that.

TIMMY. I want you to know that I overheard you and your nuthead husband saying I was adopted. I want you to know I'm so glad I am not related to either of you!

POLLY. Children! Do any of you have a child that is this rude???

ROSALIND. Mine is pretty rude. And he's one of the ones who calls Timmy Polly.

CLIFFORD. *(Wanting to move forward.)* OK. I'm going to call the police and tell them who it is doing the shooting.

POLLY. Oh poor mixed up Jimmy.

    Salena looks at the TV.

SALENA. Wait a second. They've caught the guy. *(Looks shocked.)* Oh! That isn't him, is it?

POLLY. What do you mean?

ROSALIND. God, she's right. It's not him. It's someone else.

POLLY. Oh. I'm taking this in slowly. It's not Jimmy. It's somebody else shooting people. Well what good news!

CLIFFORD. *(Looking at the TV)* Who is it then? Does anybody know?

ROSALIND. Yes he's sort of familiar. Something about lamb chops. And chopped meat. Yes. He's the butcher. He sells meat at the Stop & Shop.

TIMMY. Wow, two people in the same town decided to kill people on the same day.

POLLY. And of course Jimmy has no follow through. Just like with his novel. He only wrote three sentences. Do you want to hear them?

CLIFFORD. No I do not. Look we have this butcher person who's killing people, but Jimmy is still out there, so we've got to warn the police about him. *(Starts to dial his cell phone; frustrated.)* Uhhhhhh— I can't get a signal. Give me your phone.

POLLY. Jimmy took it with him.

CLIFFORD. Okay. I'll go outside to call the police.

POLLY. The police are awfully busy right now.

CLIFFORD. Yes they are. I'll be right back.

He exits though the door.

POLLY. Anyone want coffee?

SALENA. God, all those poor people at the mall, killed.

POLLY. Does that mean no for coffee?

Everyone stares at her.

Scene 10

Outside of the house. Clifford is already on the phone.[*]

CLIFFORD. *(Speaking into phone, talking quickly.)* …Yes, that's correct, my neighbor's name is James Peabody, and he's wearing a pillowcase on his head. What? Yes there are holes for the eyes. What? Well unfortunately we don't know where he's planning to shoot people. And his wife tells us that at an earlier time, he threatened to shoot people at a mall but then later changed his mind and drove to some river with a bridge and he threw his head…gear off the bridge into the river. Uh-huh. No the first time he was wearing a pig's head as camouflage. Yes. No not a real pig, it was a Hollywood pig. I mean *Halloween* pig.

Clifford listens briefly.

Never mind the pig's head, he's wearing a pillowcase now. Are you sure there are no policeman there I can talk to? Yes I understand they're all at the mall. Right, I understand, it's a small town. But they have arrested the man at the mall, right? So like couldn't you call up one of the cops and make him aware of this other threat. I mean this other person can still be stopped, I think. So can you call one of them?

---

[*] Note: not a real set for this, probably in a spotlight…

You don't know their cell numbers. How can you not know the cell numbers? Aren't they written down?

Uh-huh. I'm sorry—do you not work at the police station? Uh-huh. Uh-huh. Your dog is missing. Oh. And they were going to help but then there was a mass killing, and they all left, and when I called, you just answered the phone. I see.

(Irritated.) I WISH YOU HAD TOLD ME THIS EARLIER!

We've wasted a lot of time. And I guess Mr. Peabody will either kill people today or he won't. By the way, my wife and son were killed two years ago, and I often think about suicide, but I never think of killing other people at the same time. Don't you think that makes me a nice person?

    Clifford listens.

Uh-huh. Uh-huh. Well thank you for saying that.

I'm sorry, I shouldn't have said what I said. Well you're very kind. I hope you find your dog. I would help you look except I feel I need to go to a few places that Mr. Peabody may be killing people at. Oh and if you're still there when some policeman comes back, would you tell them what I said. The danger of Mr. Peabody, and he has a pillowcase on his head and lots and lots of guns.

So maybe someone could find him and stop him. Thank you. And give them my cell phone so they can call me. It's 000-000-0001. Yes it is a strange number. Life is strange.

    Clifford listens.

Thank you. Good luck to you too.

Scene 11

They are all in a car. It's a convertible. The roof is down.*
Salena is driving. Polly is next to her. Clifford, Timmy and
Rosalind are in the big seat. They are quiet and concerned.

POLLY. *(Starts to sing.)* "See the USA, in your Chevrolet, America is asking you to drive."

SALENA. What is that you're singing?

POLLY. Oh some old commercial. It just popped into my head because we're in a convertible. I've always wanted a convertible, they're so spacious.

ROSALIND. It's terrible for people with skin cancer.

POLLY. Oh give it a rest, would you? You need Vitamin D, you know. And you should eat carrots. Whose car is this?

SALENA. It's my husband's. I got it with the settlement. It always reminds me of him. I should really sell it and get something else.

CLIFFORD. How much longer until we get to that bridge you say he goes to.

POLLY. Oh I don't know. Twenty minutes. Maybe four minutes. I never really paid attention to how long it took. He was always driving too fast and shouting at me.

CLIFFORD. I think maybe we wasted time going to all those other malls.

POLLY. Well he always talked about the malls, so it seemed sensible to check them out.

CLIFFORD. And your insisting that we go to Home Depot made no sense.

POLLY. You've already said that several times. And it's my belief that Jimmy thinks Home Depot *is* a mall. So I just thought we should check it out. Plus I wanted to look at new blinds for our windows, so people like you stop looking in.

---

* Note: the car needs to look like a car, but it can be made lighter, and it needs to move—probably not on tires, but on a platform that moves. Once lights come up on it, it probably should be stationary, though maybe something in the backdrop suggests movement…

CLIFFORD. Oh, so we went to Home Depot so you could shop for a while. And just forget about stopping a killing.

POLLY. You just don't understand Jimmy. If he hasn't been shooting up malls by now, he's either taking a nap on the side of the road, or he's buying another pig's head for the next time, or else he's at the bridge, planning to plunge into the water. Plus I wish you wouldn't criticize Jimmy in front of Timmy all the time. You're demonizing him.

TIMMY. I want to remind everyone I'm adopted.

POLLY. Well Jimmy and I couldn't conceive, something was wrong with my uterus and Jimmy had problems with his sperm. So one day we went into a hospital and when no one was looking, we saw this sweet little baby girl, and we took her home, and later we realized it was a boy, and so we called him Timmy.

TIMMY. You kidnapped me from a hospital?

> *Polly didn't mean to say that; what she says next is probably a lie.*

POLLY. No, dear, I was making a joke. We went to a dog shelter and got you. I love dogs. No, we went through the proper adoption system.

CLIFFORD. You stole Timmy from a hospital?

POLLY. No, I said I was making a joke. God, does no one in the car have a sense of humor?

ROSALIND. I like knock-knock jokes. Wanna hear? Knock knock. Who's there? Polly. Polly who? Polly is a great big terrifying nutcase.

POLLY. I love the word nutcase. It's very funny. Oh, look we're at the bridge! Hooray.

> *The car comes to a halt. Not realistically but maybe sound of the car stopping. Everyone gets out of the car.*

Everyone look in the river and see if a car is there.

> *They all look down front as if that's the railing of the bridge, and one can look down to see the water. They all gasp.*

SALENA. Oh my God there is a car down there.

POLLY. Yup. That's the car. He's finally gone.

> *Jimmy suddenly arrives from stage right (audience left). The*

convertible should have come in from stage left. Jimmy is not wet, and he is carrying a gun.

JIMMY. I was going to drown myself in the car but just as I put my foot on the pedal, I suddenly changed my mind and jumped out before the car plummeted downward.

POLLY. Well, all's well that ends well.

JIMMY. I was too lonely to die by myself. I missed you and Timmy.

POLLY. Ah, you missed us?

JIMMY. And now I see you brought another car.

CLIFFORD. Put your gun down.

JIMMY. Fuck you. Polly and Timmy, get in the car.

POLLY. I have an idea! Why don't we just take a nice walk?

JIMMY. Seeing you, I feel like I could go through with it this time, with you by my side. I'd have the courage to die. It's a family affair. The people from next door will have to walk home, it'll take hours, that makes me happy. Okay, Polly and Timmy, get in the car.

> *Jimmy points his gun at Polly and Timmy. Jimmy has a lot of energy, aiming guns at them and getting them to the car.*

CLIFFORD. Wait a minute. What are you doing?

JIMMY. Don't distract me. I'm trying to kill myself, so shut up or I'll shoot you.

POLLY. Darling, remember I said maybe Clifford could help you with your book? He's a writer in newspapers. So rather than kill yourself, what about if we ask him to help you write your book.

JIMMY. *(Very serious, loud and scary.)* SHUT THE FUCK UP ABOUT MY BOOK! JUST GET INTO THE FUCKING CAR, BOTH OF YOU.

> *Jimmy's extreme shouting gets Polly and Timmy very close to the car.*

POLLY. This isn't our car, dear.

JIMMY. SHUT UP!

POLLY. Plus it's a convertible. When we hit the water, we'll just float right up to the top.

JIMMY. No I'll shoot all three of us as soon as we leave the bridge.

49

POLLY. But you're a bad shot. You're always missing me.

JIMMY. I'll use the assault rifle. Multiple bullets, you don't need to be a good shot with that.

POLLY. Oh. Well I guess that's true.

JIMMY. *GET IN THE CAR.*

> *Jimmy is aiming his gun at them. Polly and Timmy get in the car. Timmy is in the back seat. Polly whispers to him.*

What did you just say to him?

POLLY. I said I was sorry.

JIMMY. Okay finally I'm going to do what I want.

> *The car should go to the left (stage right). The car should move quickly. As the car leaves the stage we hear Polly yell out "Timmy, jump now!" We then hear the car crash through the safety rails of the bridge, immediately followed by multiple gunshots, and then a big splash.*
>
> *Clifford, Salena, and Rosalind have watched in horror. Then when they hear the car go through the railing, they follow partway after the car, and then they look downward, as if looking over the railing at the river below.*
>
> *Several seconds go by with no one moving. No noise.*
>
> *Suddenly Timmy comes in from left (stage right). He apparently jumped out when Polly told him to.*
>
> *He looks shell-shocked. He also looks out front, at the sinking car. Suddenly the two deaths shock him.*

TIMMY. NO!

CLIFFORD. *(Taking it in.)* He didn't shoot you.

TIMMY. No. He would have. She didn't whisper "I'm sorry." She whispered "get ready to jump." She distracted him. She yelled "jump now." I did what she said. I just missed the shooting. But she didn't.

SALENA. Thank God you're all right.

TIMMY. I said such mean things to her today.

CLIFFORD. You didn't mean them.

TIMMY. But I did when I said them. I guess I take them back…

Everyone stands still. No one touches each other. Lights dim.

Scene 12

Clifford and Salena's house. Next morning.
Clifford is drinking coffee or tea. He is staring out, kind of shell-shocked. Salena comes in, in a bathrobe, carrying a cup.

SALENA. Oh I thought you would've had the news on.

CLIFFORD. I dreamt it enough, I don't think I want to see it today.

SALENA. I saw it on the kitchen TV. The butcher got the most attention. Of course, he killed a lot of people. Although Polly and Jimmy going into the river was covered briefly. And that woman found her dog.

CLIFFORD. *(Surprised in a quiet way.)* Oh, she did. That's nice.

SALENA. Is he awake yet?

CLIFFORD. I imagine he may sleep a long time.

SALENA. I'm amazed he managed to sleep at all.

CLIFFORD. Well he was tied up, and forced to get in that car, and then he managed to get out, but his two crazy parents died and are gone. They were nuts, but they were all he has. Or had.

SALENA. Poor kid. Unlucky.

CLIFFORD. Well he's lucky he's alive.

SALENA. Most of the time you act like being alive isn't such a good thing.

CLIFFORD. Yes, you're right. I do act that way. I guess I've been shell-shocked for two years.

SALENA. I didn't mean to criticize.

CLIFFORD. *(Not quite sure where this is coming from, but not hesitant.)* Would you give me a hug?

> *Salena is surprised but very quickly goes to him and hugs. It is a pretty long hug. They don't cry, but they are sharing the upset*

very fully.[*]

Timmy comes out of a bedroom (presumably), and he's maybe wearing pajamas and a bathrobe they got from next door? (or he's wearing something of Clifford's). He's interested to watch Clifford and Salena embrace. Probably his parents never hugged.

Clifford and Salena were close to letting go of the hug, and now they hear him. They don't look embarrassed or anything, they just end the hug and focus on Timmy.

Hey Timmy. Did you sleep I hope?

TIMMY. I slept really deep. When I woke I suddenly remembered what happened.

CLIFFORD. Yeah. Hard to take in.

SALENA. Uh, Timmy do you want tea or coffee? Or are you hungry?

TIMMY. They never let me have coffee.

SALENA. Okay. Want tea? Want a soda? Dr. Pepper, ginger ale.

TIMMY. Dr. Pepper. Would it be all right if I took a shower?

SALENA. Sure. Maybe I'll make eggs. Scrambled all right?

TIMMY. Yes. Thank you.

He exits.

Phone rings.

CLIFFORD. *(On phone.)* Hello? Yes this is Clifford Barlow. *(Hears something important.)* Oh, yes. Yes he is with us. Uh-huh. No we're not relatives, but his parents died in a…an upsetting way, and we live next door, and the police thought it was fine if we brought him here last night. Oh yes, my…friend Salena is here too, we live together. And it seemed the best idea to have him stay. Uh-huh. In an hour? Really, that soon. Okay. What is your name again please? Karen. Okay. Well we're here. Um see you in an hour, I guess.

Clifford listens.

Yes that's the correct address. All right. *(Hangs up.)*

---

[*] Note: the request for a hug is mostly just because of the awfulness of the previous day. There is a current of affection throughout the play between Clifford and Salena. But primarily this is a request due to the awful events…

Timmy comes back in.

TIMMY. I heard the phone call.

CLIFFORD. Yes, that was foster care calling. I guess by law you're supposed to be with them. Since you're not related to us.

TIMMY. Oh. I see.

CLIFFORD. I mean the police understood you were staying with us. They said something about foster care but I wasn't expecting to hear about it so soon.

SALENA. It seems a little abrupt.

CLIFFORD. I wonder if we can delay it.

TIMMY. Gosh what's foster care? I mean what happens with it…

CLIFFORD. I'm not sure but…if you're under 18, the state has to watch over you with other young people in your predicament, and then sometimes you're put in with a family for a while, people who work with foster care; and then sometimes they or someone else adopt you and that's more permanent than foster care…and um… gosh I wasn't thinking yet what was going to happen to you…

TIMMY. I was already adopted once, it seems.

CLIFFORD. Yes, it seems so.

TIMMY. Do you think they really kidnapped me from a hospital when I was little?

CLIFFORD. I don't know what to say. Your mother was…confusing to me.

SALENA. I don't like the idea of Timmy suddenly being with total strangers. I mean, can't he stay with us for a while?

CLIFFORD. Well we could ask. Or maybe…maybe we could adopt Timmy.

TIMMY. You're just feeling sorry for me.

CLIFFORD. I'm not feeling sorry for you. I'm…feeling sorry for myself. I've been shut down…for too long. If I help you…it'll help me. *(Sincere.)* I mean, it really would help. I do think we should adopt you. I mean, if you're okay with that.

TIMMY. I like that you don't seem crazy. Both of you don't seem crazy.

CLIFFORD. *(To Salena.)* Are you okay with this?

SALENA. I am. I think it would be great to adopt Timmy.

CLIFFORD. I'm wondering if we can convince them to let him stay here now. Rather than taking him somewhere.

SALENA. Or maybe we could apply to be foster parents? Maybe that could happen faster. And adoption could happen after that…

CLIFFORD. Yeah, that's a good place to start. I hope they're open to it…

TIMMY. Could I change my name, do you think? Jimmy/Timmy for years and years was pretty tedious.

CLIFFORD. Sure. Do you have an idea?

TIMMY. Not immediately. I just think I'd like to lose the Timmy.

SALENA. What about Timothy? More grown up, not the same sound.

TIMMY. Yeah that's possible. Although I'd rather have something really different. So it feels like starting over.

CLIFFORD. What about Robert?

TIMMY. Okay but…what else?

SALENA. Clarence?

TIMMY. I don't think so.

SALENA. Sorry. I don't know where I got Clarence.

TIMMY. That's all right. We don't have to decide today.

SALENA. Ummmm…

CLIFFORD. Would you like…Petruchio?

TIMMY. No thanks.

CLIFFORD. I was joking.

TIMMY. Oh good.

CLIFFORD. William?

TIMMY. Yeah, but then they'll call me Billy, and that's like Timmy. And I don't want that.

SALENA. What about Frodo?

TIMMY. The hobbit???

SALENA. But he's the lead and he's smart and…no I'm getting silly. Let's think of some normal names.

CLIFFORD. What about Matthew?

TIMMY. Matthew. Sort of simple. But it's nice.

CLIFFORD. It's…my middle name.

TIMMY. Oh. …I think I like it.

SALENA. I like it too.

CLIFFORD. Good. Why don't we live with that for a while.

> *In a quiet way they all look pleased. Some classical music?*
> *Lights dim.*

End of Play

AUTHOR'S NOTE

Looking back on my childhood in the '50s in New Jersey, I never worried about going to school and being shot. And I wasn't worried that I'd be killed while seeing a movie. Even when I was a teenager and went into New York City to see a movie, I never got killed. And I never got killed in a mall.

Now it's true we did worry about the atomic bomb. It was a new bomb that the Americans dropped on Japan, a way to end the war quickly...and then somehow the Russians found how to make that bomb as well. In my childhood, I was aware that the Russians might drop a bomb on us. And in my Catholic school we would practice getting underneath our desks and covering our heads.

The bomb was brought by the Russians to Cuba. And suddenly one or both superpowers were about to bomb each other. But somehow President John F. Kennedy and Khrushchev calmed down. And then when I was 13, President Kennedy was assassinated in Dallas, November 22, 1963.

Then Martin Luther King Jr. was assassinated in Memphis, April 4, 1968.

Then Robert F. Kennedy was assassinated in the Ambassador Hotel in Los Angeles, June 5, 1968.

John Lennon was worldwide-famous as a member of the Beatles and for his political activism and pacifism. He now lived in NYC doing his solo career. Alas, on the evening of December 8, 1980, Lennon had just returned from a recording studio with his wife, Yoko Ono. They got into the archway of the Dakota Apartments when he was suddenly shot and killed by a crazy man named Mark David Chapman. Chapman has been denied parole many times.

On March 30, 1981, President Ronald Reagan and three others were shot and wounded by John Hinckley Jr. as they were leaving a speaking engagement at the Washington, D.C., Hilton Hotel. Reagan got well quickly. Apparently young Hinckley had an obsessive fixation on teen actress Jodie Foster, and Hinckley was found not guilty by reason of insanity and remained under institutional psychiatric care.

On April 20, 1999, at Columbine High School, west of Littleton, Colorado, two teens went on a shooting spree, killing 13 people and wounding more than 20 others before turning their guns on themselves and committing suicide at approximately 11:19 A.M. They were seniors Dylan Klebold and Eric Harris. And they had talked and prepared for the killing for the entire year.

9/11. September 11, 2001, when the Islamic terrorist group al-Qaeda hijacked four airplanes leaving from Boston—flying the first two into New York City.

I was supposed to be in New York that day to teach at Juilliard. But my partner, John Augustine, was visiting Canada, and he called and told me to turn on the TV. I saw one airplane hit into the North tower of the World Trade Center. It felt like a horrible mistake. But then the second airplane hit the South tower, and it was clear it was not a mistake. The first tower suddenly collapsed, then so did the second tower collapse. 2,606 died in the World Trade Center; 6,000 others were injured.

The third plane crashed into the Pentagon. The fourth plane was flown toward Washington, D.C., but the passengers thwarted the hijackers and took the plane to a field in Stonycreek Township, Pennsylvania. The passengers purposely avoided many more killing by not hitting D.C. The hijackers died, as did the brave passengers.

9/11 was frightening. And over time more terrorists killed. Many were already here. But the Columbine killings were the first of American mass shootings—and it has gone on and on. It seems it is the crazy/violent American man who wants to kill many other Americans for no practical reasons... or maybe he feels unhappy and wants people to suffer and die.

I started to see more random killing on the TV news starting in 1999 and as the 2000s went on. More and more and more crazy killings, almost every three weeks! It's insane. Here are some of them.

On December 14, 2012, 20-year-old Adam Lanza shot and killed his mother at their Newtown, Connecticut, home. Adam drove to the Sandy Hook Elementary School in Newtown and in less than ten minutes he fatally shot 20 children, all between six and seven years old, as well as killing six adult staff members. Then he committed suicide by shooting himself in the head. The gun belonged to his mother, she had taught him how to use it.

June 17, 2015. Dylann Storm Roof was an American white supremacist. (What a weird name.) During a prayer service at Emanuel African Methodist Episcopal Church, Roof killed nine people, all African-Americans, including the senior pastor and state senator Clementa C. Pinckney, and injured one other person. He left. Several people identified Roof as the main suspect, he became the center of a manhunt that ended the morning after the shooting with his arrest in Shelby, North Carolina. He later confessed that he committed the shooting in the hopes of igniting a race war. He was 21 years old when he did this.

On the night of October 1, 2017, Stephen Paddock opened fire on a crowd of concertgoers at the Route 91 Harvest Music Festival on the Las Vegas Strip in Nevada. Paddock, a 64-year-old man from Mesquite, Nevada, fired more than 1,100 rounds from his suite on the 32nd floor of the Mandalay Bay Hotel, killing 58 people and leaving 851 injured—over 400 of them by gunfire and hundreds more in the ensuing panic. The shooting occurred between 10:05 and 10:15 P.M.; about an hour later, Paddock was found dead in his room from a self-inflicted gunshot wound. His motive remains unknown. The incident is the deadliest mass shooting committed by an individual in the United States.

Well isn't this a cheery Author's Note?

I was still teaching playwriting at the Juilliard School with my friend Marsha Norman. And over the years every week we would listen to new plays from our students. And as Marsha and I got to know the students more and more, we would bring in the plays we were working on. So I wrote the first scene of *Turning Off the Morning News*. There was no second scene yet. Three students read the first scene. The other seven students and Marsha and myself listened.

Jimmy the father is very depressed, and he was thinking of killing himself. Or maybe killing other people and then killing himself.

Then Jimmy's wife, Polly, talks to the audience. And she seems very happy. "He's such a sweet man." She goes into the kitchen offstage. We hear Jimmy shooting at her. She screams and comes back to the living room and says to the audience, "Thank God he's a bad shot."

Then there is Timmy, who is 13. As an author I didn't want a real 13-year-old, so I have Polly talk to the audience: "Oh here's Timmy, my son. He's in the eighth grade. He's very shy. Aren't you, Timmy? I know he looks 17 or 18, but we didn't want to cast a real 13-year-old." In school they make fun of him. Polly tries to help Timmy learn how to make friends. Her suggestions are not too helpful, however.

Then the father, Jimmy, comes in, angry, wearing a scary Halloween mask. And he has two big guns inside a big black garbage bag. And he says he's going to kill many people in the mall today and then kill himself. And then he drives away.

Timmy is scared and wants to call the police, but Polly insists that the police are too busy. And besides, Jimmy's Halloween mask is just a joke; he is playing with them. Polly changes to other topics, while Timmy is feeling caught with these parents.

So that was what my students heard, and they were very encouraging.

But I didn't know what to do next for a while.

Then a month later I decided I wanted to have a couple next door to Jimmy and Polly. And the new people were NOT crazy. I wanted two normal characters who are friends and just moved into the house recently—Salena and Clifford. Salena recently divorced her husband. A while ago, Clifford had a tragedy in his family.

I also thought of a sixth character named Rosalind, who meets Salena and they become friends. Rosalind is also divorced, and she has a son who is a bit of a bully, like her husband. She is eccentric in many ways—especially the way she wears a pillowcase on her head when she is outside. She likes to explain that she had many basal cells, due to the sun. And she had to have "Mohs surgery" many times to take off the cells on her face or neck. (Rosalind explains it to Salena, and thus to the audience.)

So I finished my first draft, and showed it to Emily Mann at McCarter Theatre. I've known Emily for many years. She is a playwright and director and actress. We first met at Harvard in a small play-writing seminar. The wonderful teacher was William Alfred. He was a professor of English literature at Harvard. And in the '60s he wrote plays—his most famous play was *Hogan's Goat*, starring Faye Dunaway. This was Faye Dunaway's first success, and she would go to Cambridge to visit Professor Alfred at Harvard. These visits continued when she had her first big movie success, *Bonnie and Clyde*. Many, including myself, would see Ms. Dunaway going to Mr. Alfred's house near the Harvard Houses. I was in Dunster House near the river.

Sorry, I am getting older and remembering more and more and more things. Isn't that delightful. Okay let me go back to Emily and me.

We liked each other's plays at the Harvard seminar. She was in her first year, and had three more years to go. I was in my last, fourth, year.

Then to my relief and surprise I got into the Yale School of Drama, where I was happy working with wonderful actors and teachers. I started to hear of Emily's plays in New York and elsewhere. And at Yale I had become friends with Wendy Wasserstein.

And then Wendy became friends with Emily, and then Emily asked Wendy if she could write a play for the McCarter. Wendy said she was doing too many projects already, and Wendy suggested Emily should call me and see if I would write a play for McCarter.

And I said yes. And then Emily and I became good friends, and over time I wrote three plays for Emily and the McCarter: *Miss Witherspoon*, *Vanya and Sonia and Masha and Spike*; and now this new play, *Turning Off the Morning News*.

Miss Witherspoon, which had a double premiere at McCarter Theatre and Playwrights Horizons (featuring Kristine Nielsen), was a finalist for the 2006 Pulitzer Prize.

Vanya and Sonia and Masha and Spike had a double premiere at McCarter Theatre and Lincoln Center. Then it moved to Broadway thanks to Joey Parnes and Larry Hirschhorn and many others, and Emily Mann for McCarter and André Bishop for Lincoln Center. It won the 2013 Tony Award for Best Play. This play also won Best Play from the New York Drama Critics' Circle, the Drama Desk Award, the Outer Critics Circle, the Drama League Award, and the Off-Broadway Alliance Award. *Vania and Sonia* was a play that ended up happy, to my total surprise.

Emily asked me to do another play. I showed her the first four scenes. Then I did the first draft. And we had a reading of *Turning Off the Morning News*. We had an audience, and excellent actors. Readings are very helpful.

I did another draft which we both liked. Just like the previous two plays, Emily wanted to put the play at the McCarter, and then work with a New York theater as well.

The first theater said yes, which felt good; but about three weeks later, it turned out that the schedule for two-years-plus made producing it impossible. So we went to another Off-Broadway theater that said yes. And we worked with them on changes and casting over two months. But the money for this production fell through, and it just couldn't work.

So then we showed it to another theater who likes my work but was bothered by the topic. They felt it should be serious only. I could see what they felt. But I wanted the play to be unusual, comic, upsetting, serious, and I wanted to make the ending somewhat hopeful.

So Emily decided to put the play at the McCarter by itself. And then we chose six terrific actors: Jimmy was John Pankow, Polly was Kristine Nielsen, Timmy was Nicholas Podany, Clifford was Robert Sella, Salena was Rachel Nicks, and Rosalind was Jenn Harris.

I saw John Pankow in the early '80s in a play called *Forty-Deuce*, where John and others played young hustlers. The others were scary but he was funny. Later he and I were cast in the movie *The Secret of My Success*. Later still, in my play *Why Torture Is Wrong, and the People Who Love Them* John was cast as a strange Reverend Mike. And in this new play *Turning Off the Morning News*, John played the scary man Jimmy who wants to kill people at the mall and himself; or maybe his family; or perhaps finish his novel.

Kristine Nielsen and I also became friends in the '80s. We both had small roles in a terrible production of *Ubu* at Lincoln Center. Then she was cast as the crazy mother, Mrs. Seismograph, in my play *Betty's Summer Vacation*, and she won an Obie award. She was in seven more of my plays including *Miss Witherspoon*, and she received a Tony nomination for *Vanya and Sonia and Masha and Spike*. In *Turning Off the Morning News* Kristine played Polly, another crazy, oblivious mother, who is longing for heaven where she believes there is a red carpet waiting for her.

Nicholas Podany played Timmy. We met when I was teaching playwriting at Juilliard. The Juilliard actors would work once a week reading in or observing the new plays by the playwriting students. Nicholas was asked to read several students' work and I was very impressed with him. Later, when Emily Mann wanted to have a reading of this play, I suggested that Nicholas play Timmy. He got permission from Juilliard that day. Timmy is scared of his father; his mother talks endlessly. As Timmy feels his parents have gone crazy, the neighbors seem to help Timmy more. Anyway, Nicholas got to be in the full production. I think he is very talented. (And recently he was in *Harry Potter* on Broadway.)

Robert Sella played Clifford, who has just moved to a new place, getting away from some misfortunes. His friend Salena got divorced, and she and Clifford are now sharing a house. I also knew Robert in Juilliard—he was nice and talented. He played a mix of a woman and man in *The Adventures of Herculina* by Kira Obolensky, one of my favorite playwrights. Robert soon finished at Juilliard, and then he went to Broadway in *Sylvia*, *My Fair Lady*, *Chitty Chitty Bang Bang*, *Angels in America*. And Dame Maggie Smith was in *The Lady from Dubuque* with Robert in the West End.

Rachel Nicks played Salena. She also went to Juilliard. And that means there were three talented actors from Juilliard. Rachel played Salena, who tried to help Cliff about not being so worried. And Salena and Rosalind became friends. They decided it was good to meet with the neighbors. But it turned into not a good idea. Rachel was in *Skeleton Crew* at the Old Globe. Her Off-Broadway credits include Branden Jacobs-Jenkins' *War* at LCT3, Naomi Wallace's *And I and Silence* at Signature Theatre and *The Good Negro* by Tracey Scott Wilson at the Public.

Jenn Harris played Rosalind, with a pillowcase on her head for fear of the sun. Jenn is very funny. Off-Broadway: *Modern Orthodox* (Lucille Lortel Award and then the Theatre World Award). Her web series, *New York Is Dead*, which she co-wrote, starred in, and produced premiered at the Tribeca Film Festival in 2017, won Best Comedy at the NYTVF.

Some miscellaneous thoughts:

For the McCarter, original music and sound design was made by Mark Bennett. Emily and I have worked with Mark many times. In rehearsal the sound of guns was too loud and scary. Mark brought it down a lot. You don't want the audience to hurt their ears. (The music is very good, and you could check into licensing it through Patrick Herold at ICM Partners.)

The character of Jimmy is tricky. He can't be played scary, although he is "off" and gets annoyed and/or angry at Polly. For a while he decides he wants to make a book, and Polly tries to help him.

At McCarter the final scene with Timmy and Clifford and Salena seemed to make the audience relax a bit. Me too.

—Christopher Durang
2019

PROPERTY LIST
(Use this space to create props lists for your production)

SOUND EFFECTS
(Use this space to create sound effects lists for your production)

Dear reader,

Thank you for supporting playwrights by purchasing this acting edition! You may not know that Dramatists Play Service was founded, in 1936, by the Dramatists Guild and a number of prominent play agents to protect the rights and interests of playwrights. To this day, we are still a small company committed to our partnership with the Guild, and by proxy all playwrights, established and aspiring, working in the English language.

Because of our status as a small, independent publisher, we respectfully reiterate that this text may not be distributed or copied in any way, or uploaded to any file-sharing sites, including ones you might think are private. Photocopying or electronically distributing books means both DPS and the playwright are not paid for the work, and that ultimately hurts playwrights everywhere, as our profits are shared with the Guild.

We also hope you want to perform this play! Plays are wonderful to read, but even better when seen. If you are interested in performing or producing the play, please be aware that performance rights must be obtained through Dramatists Play Service. This is true for *any* public perfomance, even if no one is getting paid or admission is not being charged. Again, playwrights often make their sole living from performance royalties, so performing plays without paying the royalty is ultimately a loss for a real writer.

This acting edition is the **only approved text for performance**. There may be other editions of the play available for sale from other publishers, but DPS has worked closely with the playwright to ensure this published text reflects their desired text of all future productions. If you have purchased a revised edition (sometimes referred to as other types of editions, like "Broadway Edition," or "[Year] Edition"), that is the only edition you may use for performance, unless explicitly stated in writing by Dramatists Play Service.

Finally, this script cannot be changed without written permission from Dramatists Play Service. If a production intends to change the script in any way—including casting against the writer's intentions for characters, removing or changing "bad" words, or making other cuts however small—without permission, they are breaking the law. And, perhaps more importantly, changing an artist's work. Please don't do that!

We are thrilled that this play has made it into your hands. We hope you love it as much as we do, and thank you for helping us keep the American theater alive and vital.

Note on Songs/Recordings, Images, or Other Production Design Elements

Be advised that Dramatists Play Service, Inc., neither holds the rights to nor grants permission to use any songs, recordings, images, or other design elements mentioned in the play. It is the responsibility of the producing theater/organization to obtain permission of the copyright owner(s) for any such use. Additional royalty fees may apply for the right to use copyrighted materials.

For any songs/recordings, images, or other design elements mentioned in the play, works in the public domain may be substituted. It is the producing theater/organization's responsibility to ensure the substituted work is indeed in the public domain. Dramatists Play Service, Inc., cannot advise as to whether or not a song/arrangement/recording, image, or other design element is in the public domain.

NOTES

(Use this space to make notes for your production)

NOTES
(Use this space to make notes for your production)

NOTES

(Use this space to make notes for your production)